Hypnosis with the Hard to Hypnotise

Hypnosis with the Hard to Hypnotise

by Graham Old

Hypnosis with the Hard to Hypnotise

Copyright © GRAHAM OLD

First published 2018 by Plastic Spoon

The right of Graham Old to be identified as the author of this Work has been asserted by him in accordance with sections 77 and 78 of the Copyright, Designs and Patents Act 1988.

All rights reserved. No part of this publication may be reproduced, stored in a retrieval system, copied in any form or by any means, electronic, mechanical, photocopying, recording or otherwise transmitted without written permission from the publisher. You must not circulate this book in any format.

Thank you for respecting the hard work of the author and the Brief Hypnosis team.

Preface

The book you are now reading is the sixth title in our ongoing *Inductions Masterclass* series.

Our general aim for the books in the series has been that they will act as useful introductions to the wider workings of hypnosis by extracting valuable insights from the practice of specific inductions. However, this book is a little different.

Whilst most of the other books in this series have taken a single induction and used it as the context for teaching ideas and practices that are helpful for the wider use of hypnosis, this book actually presents a number of inductions. In fact, the book itself is not specifically about an induction, or even a group of inductions. Instead, this book explores an area that appears to cause a great deal of trouble, as well as more than a little trepidation, for those seeking to hypnotise others. I am talking of the experience of working with clients who may appear resistant, analytical, or otherwise hard to hypnotise.

In some ways, this book may seem to be more theoretical than its companion volumes. It certainly spends some time unpacking ideas, as well as refuting models and methodologies that may be commonly accepted by others. However, it is hoped that the number of inductions that are discussed, even if some are only mentioned in passing, will more than even out the theory-practical balance. In effect, other books in the series aimed to teach an induction and unpacked that induction to show some of the principles contained within. This book aims to teach some principles and uses inductions to demonstrate those principles in action.

This book originally began some years ago as an exploration of the Confusion induction, building upon ideas first introduced in *The Hypnotic Handshakes*. Yet, as

I delved deeper into the induction – both through ongoing reflective practice and academic research – I became increasingly uncomfortable with much that was written and practised in the name of confusion. Additionally, as my own private practice continued to increasingly attract clients that might be described as analytical, I was compelled to reconsider my own understanding of and approach to such people. The fruit of my studies, practical experience and re-thinking is the book you are now reading.

As with the other books in the series, we are again aiming to duplicate the level, detail and quality of information you might receive at a live training. So, we aim to provide in-depth practical information, point to useful theoretical discussions, anticipate questions from 'the Floor' and handle natural diversions and meandering discussions along the way.

My hope is that this book will equip the reader to welcome the previously 'hard to hypnotise,' drop any fears or preconceptions, and enjoy the experience of working with some fascinating people.

The chapter 'Responding to Resistance' contains sections that originally appeared in my earlier book, *My Friend John*. The chapter 'Rethinking Confusion' is largely based on a journal article that I wrote for REFRAME Magazine and is reprinted with permission.

Acknowledgements

I am forever grateful for my clients, particularly those who challenged me and stuck with my whilst I learned the most effective ways to work with them. Thank you for your patience and continued inspiration!

All Rights Reserved

Except where otherwise stated, intellectual property rights and copyright are retained by Graham Old. Please do not copy any portion of this work without explicit permission from the author.

Disclaimer

We are offering a model for consideration, investigation and conversation. No part of this work is meant as a replacement for proper training in effective hypnosis or psychotherapy.

Please be aware that any experimentation with the ideas presented in this document is undertaken at your own risk and responsibility. At all times when practising hypnosis, it is your responsibility to ensure that you comply with the laws and regulations of your home country, region, state or territory.

Contents

Introduction	11
Why are People Hard to Hypnotise?	19
Outline of a Pre-talk	25
Responding to Resistance	29
Mary, Mary, Quite Contrary	47
The Auto Dual Induction Transcript	59
The Myth of the Analytical Subject	65
Transcript of Sensory Overlap	91
Confusion	99
Typical Confusion Induction Transcript	113
How to Use Confusion	119
Rethinking Confusion	129
Kinaesthetic Confusion Transcript	139
Phenomenal Inductions	145
Becoming More Hypnotic	167
Fractionation Conversation Transcript	181
Summary	195
FAQ and Troubleshooting	201
Appendix A - Therapeutic Story-telling	219
Appendix B - Autism Resources	221
Bibliography	225
About the Author	231

GRAHAM OLD

Introduction

All hypnotists will have occasions when they struggle to work with someone. They may feel that they cannot get any real rapport with their client, or fail to build any expectation with them, or even sense that they are unable to hold their client's interest, or absorb their attention in any meaningful way.

This, in itself, is not particularly significant, or even all that troublesome. It simply is the way things are. As they say, you cannot win them all. However, it becomes another issue if the hypnotist notices that it is always a particular type of client that causes them problems. They may struggle to work effectively with people older than them, or fail to gain any rapport with clients of the opposite sex, or they may find that they never seem to achieve much when working with children. Although it may not seem like it at the time, such a situation can be a valuable one. It highlights a gap in knowledge or experience that the hypnotist can be grateful for, inspiring them to go out and learn some more skills.

Nevertheless, there is one group of people that many hypnotists either struggle with, or presume they will do and therefore avoid like the plague. Over the years, this group have acquired the dubious reputation of being notoriously difficult to hypnotise. They are mentioned in hypnosis trainings, with warnings and precautions aplenty. So ingrained is the belief that this group are difficult to hypnotise that their poor reputation is rarely questioned. As a result, hypnotists may not be as inclined to develop their skills to work with this group – as they might be with, for example, children – instead falling back on the presumption of difficulty and simply praying that it is some time before they encounter another member of this group.

I am talking, of course, of those clients who are often labelled resistant, or analytical.

The Hard to Hypnotise

It might be useful to explain why we have chosen the description that we have. Why did we not just refer to these people with some of the more common terms, such as resistant patients, analytical subjects, or difficult clients? The fact is that each of these labels make assumptions about the client, often judging their motives and then effectively placing the blame for the failure to achieve hypnosis squarely on the client's shoulders. This is not an approach we are comfortable sharing.

All too often, hypnotists who encounter someone they cannot hypnotise jump to all kinds of assumptions. They seem to instantly acquire the ability to read minds and know with great confidence that their client is resistant to change, or is bound by fear, or is refusing to "give-in." The client is effectively being a poor hypnotee and the hypnotist aims to find some way to address that so that they can carry on with business as usual.

We view things slightly differently. If a hypnotist is

struggling to hypnotise someone, the most that can be said at that point in time is that the hypnotist is struggling to hypnotise them! We do not know, unless we are explicitly told, that the client is resisting the hypnotist. Even if our client proudly tells us that they are "an analytical," we do not know that their instinctive analysis is the reason why hypnosis is not happening. All we can say with any certainty is that, from the perspective of the hypnotist that client is currently hard to hypnotise.

It seems to me that one of the worst things we can do with clients who may appear to be analytical, or whom we might assume to be resistant, is to expect the worst. For, no matter how hard we may try to hide it, such a low expectation will be clearly picked-up by our client. Such clients may have had other hypnotists fail to hypnotise them, or have been told that they are difficult or even impossible to hypnotise. They may have come to us with their last shred of hope, desperate to find someone who could work with them. And the minute they look in our eyes, they will know whether we think we can work with them or not.

One of the mostly unspoken requests that this book will make of you is to approach each client as an individual. I am sure that if you find that your usual tools and techniques are not working with someone, you adapt what you are doing to find something that does work. In the same way, I hope to encourage you to develop a new level of flexibility when working with people who might seem to be analytical-thinkers, or who appear to be resistant in some way. I aim to provoke hypnotists to up-skill themselves to learn new ways of working with clients they may have previously feared or even written-off.

Much of this book is theoretical, because I have found it necessary to question and challenge much of the language, attitudes and approaches that come up when faced with clients who are hard to hypnotise. It is time to move away from the fear, judgement and labelling of the past, that so often accompanied such clients. It is time instead for us to welcome clients who may respond slightly differently to the majority, embracing the learning opportunity and enjoying the privilege of working with those who put their trust in us.

Where are we Heading?

We will examine the concept of the resistant client and present an alternative understanding of resistance. We will make the argument for a more interactional perspective of the hypnotic encounter and offer some suggestions on how to proceed when there seems to be resistance in the interaction.

We will follow this by talking about a subset of resistant clients, known in NLP circles as "polarity responders." We will challenge such labelling of clients, whilst providing some ideas on a useful way to work with such people. This will be followed by a transcript of the Auto Dual Induction, as one example of an approach that may prove to be effective with this client group.

The other type of client who is often grouped together with the apparently resistant client is the so-called analytical. We will examine the concept of the analytical subject, suggesting that the label is both routinely misapplied – in that it is used too inclusively and applied too liberally – and that even when the label does apply, it is not appropriate. We will spend some time questioning the pigeon-holing of clients and whether such static descriptions really do justice to the people who seek to work with us.

We will then consider some principles to bear in mind when working with so-called analytical subjects. Some of these principles will be seen in the transcript of a Sensory Overlap induction.

Confusion is very often seen as the go-to approach when working with resistant or analytical clients. We will discuss the nature and function of confusion at length. I will also include a transcript of a typical Confusion induction, as an example of the common approach. I will then break down exactly how confusion can be used in an induction, relying on the extensive work of Stephen Gilligan in this area. Finally, I will then completely question everything I have said about confusion, sharing why I now use it in very limited ways!

We will then turn to the question of phenomena, which I will argue is the key to working with the client-base that we are discussing. I will provide a number of examples of phenomenal inductions, arguing that phenomena is far more effective, therapeutic and respectful than confusion.

Following this, there will be a discussion around the question of being more hypnotic – both for practitioners and clients. Some tips, techniques and learning exercises are provided to potentially increase hypnotic response.

As with the other books in this series, we will end with a Frequently Asked Questions section. This is mostly derived from questions that I have been asked when presenting this material in trainings, as well as online, in personal correspondence and – quite frankly – in my own imagination.

There are numerous exercises to be completed throughout the book, to practically reinforce the information presented within. These are presented as an essential element of the book, not an optional extra. It is suggested that you take part in these with what teachers of Zen call a 'Beginner's Mind' – humbly enjoying the experience of learning and experiencing something new.

Terminology used

Throughout this book you will find us referring to 'trance' and at times using terminology such as 'subconscious', deepening, being 'under' hypnosis and so on. Please bear in mind that these are purely phenomenological descriptions, merely meant to convey what the hypnotee may be experiencing. We are not endorsing any particular interpretation of hypnosis, or taking sides in the perennial debates over the nature of trance or the existence of a special hypnotic state.

For more on our experiential model of hypnosis, which fits comfortably with all the major schools of Hypnosis, see our book, *Therapeutic Inductions.*

EXERCISE

Think about times when you have found it difficult to be hypnotised.

Perhaps the first time someone hypnotised you, you did not know what to expect. Or, maybe there have been times when you could not seem to get in the right-frame of mind to be hypnotised.

If you cannot think of an example, think of times when you have found it difficult to enter into trance, whether that was relaxing, concentrating, exercising, or even getting off to sleep.

Have there been times when it felt like your mind just would not "play ball"? What was that like for you?

GRAHAM OLD

HYPNOSIS WITH THE HARD TO HYPNOTISE

Why are People Hard to Hypnotise?

An initial step in working with someone who appears to be hard to hypnotise is to carefully consider our words. If we accept, for now, the proposition that in an interaction between a hypnotist and a client, the client may appear to be "hard to hypnotise," why might this be?

A revealing key as to why some people may struggle can be seen in the language we use. If we say that someone is "hard to hypnotise," we are seemingly speaking of a scenario where one person (the hypnotist) is attempting to do something (hypnosis) to someone else (the client). This is an interaction with a *clear* power imbalance and it would not be surprising to learn that the root of the problem is that the client is opposing the imposition of someone else's will. A more collaborative approach would likely achieve a markedly different result.

In fact, as simple as this one notion might be, I would suggest that it may be at the heart of a great number of unsuccessful attempts to hypnotise someone. At the very least, it should give us some serious pause for thought. It may well be that a reconsideration of how we present ourselves and the entire hypnotic endeavour could have a dramatic effect on our interactions with others.

A common hurdle to be overcome – though it can be overcome simply enough – is that of fear. This can take a number of forms. It may refer to the client's fear that they will be made to do something they do not wish to do. It may be a fear that they will, for example, reveal their deepest secrets under hypnosis, as though it were a truth serum. They may not fully trust the hypnotist and thus feel vulnerable and unsafe in their presence. Similarly, they may be anxious about giving up control, particularly to someone they have just met.

Another possibility to explain a failed interaction is a misunderstanding as to the nature of hypnosis. This goes beyond the fears spoken of above. Someone may presume that from the moment they close their eyes, they will hear nothing but the hypnotist's voice. If this is not the case, they may presume the hypnosis is not working, or even that they cannot be hypnotised. Related to this point is the client who is unsure of their role in the hypnotic process. They may be unclear as to how passive or active they should be, perhaps attempting to help the hypnotist or make things happen.

Of course, as hypnosis is an interactional process, we cannot only assume that the 'blame' for 'failure' to achieve hypnosis lies with the client. At times, the hypnotist may be using the completely wrong approach with the person in front of them. They may be lacking the skills and knowledge to hypnotise this particular client. Or, there may be some other tension between client and hypnotist that explains the lack of harmony between them. Perhaps there is a cultural clash and the client feels judged in some way by the hypnotist. Or the client may object to being hypnotised by someone younger than them, or of the opposite gender, for example.

HYPNOSIS WITH THE HARD TO HYPNOTISE

Can They Be Hypnotised?

Some schools of thought teach that not everyone can be hypnotised. However, this is not a position held by the author. In my experience, those who believe that some people can not be hypnotised are more likely to meet such people than those who do not. Again, taking an interactional perspective, all that can be said is that a particular hypnotist has not managed to hypnotise a particular 'subject' in a particular way on a particular occasion.

It may be that some people – either due to innate ability or circumstantial context – are more hypnotisable than others. The 20th century saw the development of a number of hypnotic susceptibility scales, which aimed to measure hypnotic suggestibility reliably. These scales gauge a person's susceptibility to hypnosis as 'high', 'medium,' or 'low.' A commonly cited statistic states that roughly 80% of the population are medium, 10% are high and 10% are low. So, it may be the case that we should expect 10% of the people that we attempt to hypnotise to be difficult to work with.

There is no agreement amongst researchers on whether their scales measure an innate hypnotic trait that someone has, or their current hypnotic skill-level. Thus, some see the 10/80/10 scale of low, high and medium as a fixed trait, whilst other see it as a changeable hypnotic skill-level.

We will spend a later chapter discussing how to help clients increase their hypnotisability, so I suppose my position on this debate is clear. Even amongst those who see hypnotisability as an innate trait, there is generally an acknowledgement that certain things such as expectancy and inductions, as well as the simple act of labelling an event as hypnosis, can have a modest impact on the level of hypnotisability. So, if they accept that a modest change is possible, even if it is temporary, then this opens the door to the idea that the degree to which someone responds can be modified.

Most researchers use the term 'hypnotisability' to refer to a subject's ability to positively respond to suggestions given in hypnosis. However, this is a fairly superficial description. It does not address what is involved in responding to such suggestions. I would suggest that at least the following four factors are usually involved:

- Capacity for involuntary/subconscious response
- Imagination / fantasy ability
- Ability to become absorbed in mental processes
- Dissociative capacity

If someone responds well in those four areas, it would seem to classify them as highly hypnotisable. On the other hand, if they appear to lack in those areas, they would likely be considered to be a 'low' hypnotisabe person.

The interesting thing about these scales for our purposes is how they apply, or rather do not apply, to many of those people considered hard to hypnotise. Let's leave for the time-being those who may be genuinely 'low' in their natural capacity for hypnosis, knowing that we will return in a later chapter to discuss ways to assist lows to become highs. For now, I simply want to make the point that there is no reason to assume that 'analytical resisters'[1] are lacking in either of the four factors discussed above. As but one example, those who are highly analytical might be understood to often find themselves absorbed in their own thought processes. That would seem to be as good a description of what it means to be analytical as anything else!

If this point stands, then it would mean that if we find ourselves struggling to hypnotise an analytical client, or find ourselves thinking that a client is resisting hypnosis for some reason, there is no reason to conclude that we will not be able to hypnotise them. We simply need to adjust our approach, just as we would with anyone else who did not seem to be responding to the first thing we tried.

---

[1] This is one of the dreadful umbrella terms often used to group resistant clients and analytical subjects together.

EXERCISE

Are there any people, or groups of people that you find it difficult to hypnotise?

If you have not yet encountered this, are there any people, or groups of people that you are slightly nervous about working with?

Do the difficulties that you experience – or envisage experiencing – seem insurmountable? Or can they be lessened with further training, education, or experience?

Outline of a Pre-talk

The following outline is not a script to follow, or an exact replica of how I work. After all, no one wants to see lots of little clones of Graham Old running around! However, this is fairly close to the sort of model I often use and serves of a useful example of things you may want to include.

This is explicitly not offered as *the* only way to deliver a pre-talk. After all, you might notice that this differs significantly from the example provided in my book on the Elman Induction.[2] As with the majority of the content in this book – and the other books in this series – this is provided as an example to provoke discussion and practical experimentation.

Hypnotherapists often use the pre-talk to address any fears that their clients may have. However, it is important to ensure that in the process they are not installing any fears that did not previously exist.

An area that may deserve fresh consideration is the over-reliance on pre-scripted information to be shared during the pre-talk. It is understandable that hypnotherapists will want to ensure that all important

---

[2] The pre-talk provided in *The Elman Induction* served to demonstrate a way to frame that induction, particularly if working from an Elmanian perspective.

information is recalled. However, reliance on a formal script can inhibit freedom and flexibility.

It seems to me that rather than having a pre-scripted pre-talk it is preferable to simply have a conversation with your clients. Rather than listing all of the potential fears that someone may have, to then address these one-by-one, why not ask a natural question like, "So, how are you feeling about experiencing hypnosis?"

Paying attention to what your client says, as well as their body language when doing so, will provide you with plenty of information to proceed with. Similarly, asking, "Is there anything you're not sure about?" gives your client the option to raise any fears they may have without necessarily implying that they should have some.

This is not to say that you can not possibly have any notes or pointers with you. However, I would encourage using this time to have a dialogue, rather than delivering a one-way lecture.

HYPNOSIS WITH THE HARD TO HYPNOTISE

Outline of a Pre-talk

1) Have you experienced Hypnosis before?

- If negative, discuss. Explain your approach is different
- If positive, discuss expectations. Congratulate them on their hypnotic ability
- If no:

2) So, how are you feeling about experiencing hypnosis?

- Discuss any concerns / misconceptions that arise

2b) Is there anything you're not sure about?

- Discuss any concerns / misconceptions that arise

3) <u>Experiential</u> explanation

- Compare hypnosis to a day-dream (including the common experience of varieties of depth in dreams). Describe this as a natural capacity of the human brain
- Cinema comparison – we focus and choose to lose ourselves in an alternate reality
- Include phenomena to aid the explanation and preview what is to come.

4) Shall we do this?

EXERCISE

What do you feel should be included in a good pre-talk?

Do you think it is better to address common fears and misconceptions, or wait to see what the client brings up?

Do you prefer the idea of working with a pre-written pre-talk, or an impromptu one?

Outline your own pre-talk, noting any essentials that you think should be included.

Responding to Resistance

Some time ago, I was perusing an online hypnosis forum. One participant was asking for advice with a client that they found particularly tricky. If I recall correctly, they were attempting to use the Elman induction, but could not achieve eye-closure. Apparently, their client would insist on opening their eyes, either when told they could not, or if they heard a disturbing sound, sensed a light flicker and so on.

The first person to respond to this questioner was supposedly a hypnotist with some experience. Their response was firm and swift:

"They are resisting. Fire them as a client."

I found this response puzzling and disturbing for a number of reasons. Firstly, *even if* the client was resisting, is it really our best course of action to "fire them" at the first sign of resistance? Is there not a better way to proceed in such a situation?

Secondly, can we really assume that someone is "resisting" if they do not respond to our every command? Are there really no other factors that may be in play? I once worked with a female client who had been raped by someone who glued her eyes shut. I'm not suggesting that anything like that was a consideration here, but it at least demonstrates that an assumption of resistance may be a leap.

Much of what follows in this chapter has previously been addressed in the other books in this series. However, I believe that it bears repeating. In fact, it seems to me that this may be the most important chapter in this book. At the very least, I hope to challenge the therapist-centred outlook which presumes that any time a client does not do exactly as requested, they are "resisting." This strikes me as a shallow self-serving presumption unfitting of anyone claiming to be any kind of therapist.

Every single client who does us the honour of choosing to work with us is a uniquely complex individual. It would be possible for them to display exactly the same kind of behaviour as the client we encountered before them, but for completely different reasons. To presume that any time someone does not do exactly as we requested they must be resisting seems to me to be a massive misunderstanding of hypnosis *and* human nature.

As Kelley T. Woods recently wrote:

> The truth is that any client who has bothered to book an appointment with a hypnosis practitioner, shows up on time and is prepared to pay the fee is hardly resistant. Especially for those who have suffered chronic issues such as pain, anxiety or other debilitating problems, the desire for relief and improvement is immense.[3]

---

3 Kelley T. Woods, "Myth of the Resistant Client," *Reframe Magazine*, p. 11.

HYPNOSIS WITH THE HARD TO HYPNOTISE

In short, Resistance is not a useful concept. It implies that the client does not want to change, which may in fact be contrary to all evidence. It is surely better to approach the client from a position of cooperation than from a position of resistance, power and control.

This is not to say that hypnotists will never encounter a client who does not respond as expected, or desired. However, what it does mean is that the assumption of resistance on the part of such clients is neither justified, nor beneficial. It is an outdated concept and an unhelpful presumption. There has to be a more useful, productive and generous way to approach such situations.

Rethinking Resistance

Steve de Shazer, one of the pioneers of Solution-Focused Brief Therapy, published an important article in 1984, entitled *'The Death of Resistance.'* In the article, de Shazer argues that the concept of resistance is a bad idea and a hindrance to therapists. According to him, what works better is to view therapy as a process of cooperation between therapist and client. Resistance is therefore seen as a unique way of cooperating.

De Shazer proposed that everything the client says or does can best be seen as an attempt to help the therapy process move forward. When the client says or does something the therapist does not understand right away, the therapist should not confront the client. Instead, the therapist should assume that the client had a good reason for saying or doing what they did. Approaching the client creatively and constructively in this way is thought to help build cooperation.

Robert Wubbolding, director of training for the William Glasser Institute and director of the Centre for Reality Therapy also has a similarly positive take on resistance. He writes that, "It is a client's best attempt to meet their needs, especially their need for power or accomplishment."

Ten years after his initial article on the subject, de Shazer wrote a follow-up piece entitled, 'Resistance Revisited.' In that article, de Shazer wrote of the evolution that the concept of resistance goes through:

> A funny thing happens to concepts over time. No matter how useful any concept might be at the start, eventually they all seem to become reified. Instead of remaining explanatory metaphors, they become facts. That is, rather than saying "it is as if the client is resisting change," once reified, people begin to say things like "the client is resisting" and eventually they begin to say that "resistance exists and must be sought out." At this point, the concept has outlived its usefulness and needs to be gotten rid of because, once reified, it can never again be a metaphor.[4]

So, resistance is a nominalisation: taking a process, or a verb, and making it into a noun. And de Shazer is surely correct in saying that in this instance, it is not a helpful

---

4 S. de Shazer, *Resistance Revisited* in Contemporary Family Therapy (1989) 11: 227. See also, de Shazer, (1984), *The Death of Resistance*. Family Process, 23: 11–17.

nominalisation.

Clifton Mitchell, a professor and coordinator of the counselling program at East Tennessee State University, defines resistance as something "created when the method of influence is mismatched with the client's current propensity to accept the manner in which the influence is delivered." This would support the idea that resistance is something that takes place within the interaction of the client and therapist, not a characteristic of specific clients.

Yvonne Dolan writes:

> It is well known among experienced clinicians that rigidly expecting a client to change at the therapist's rate, rather than according to the client's own internal rhythms and personal abilities, is tantamount to setting that person up to fail.[5]

This suggests that resistance happens when we expect or push for change when the client is not ready for that change, or is not ready to receive the impetus to change in the way we are delivering it. That unreadiness may be a result of fear, or simply because they do not understand what is taking place. In a hypnotic context, it may be because they do not understand their role in the process.

In that sense, resistance may very well exist. Yet, it is not our place to assume that it exists *within the client*. The most we can say is that resistance is present in the interaction. It is not therefore something that exists in a

---

5 Y. M. Dolan, (1985). *A Path With a Heart: Ericksonian utilization with resistant and chronic clients.* New York: Brunner/Mazel. p. 20

client in a static sense. After all, as Michael Yapko reminds us, 'When there are two people (or more) in an interaction, there is a shared responsibility for the outcome.'[6]

Working with Resistance

When we do encounter resistant statements or behaviour, it is easy to fall into a pattern of arguing or to push back. In such a scenario, it is as if the client and the therapists are in a tug of war with each pulling harder on his end of the rope in order to drag the other across the line into submission. This is a guaranteed way to take the client's resistant behaviour and multiply it by our own resistant response to that behaviour, resulting in an increased experience of resistance and frustration in the interaction.

The Motivational Interviewing approach to counselling employs the useful idea of "rolling with resistance." Rolling with Resistance is a key technique which recognises that simply attacking or confronting someone directly does not usually work. In fact, it may do little more than drive people deeper into their shell or lead them to be increasingly defensive or confrontational.

As Milton Erickson wrote:

> Resistance should be openly accepted, in fact, graciously accepted, since it is a vitally important communication of a part of their problems and often can be used as an opening

---
6 Michael Yapko, *Essentials of Hypnosis*, p. 220.

into their defenses.[7]

As we have suggested in a number of books, the martial art of Aikido can teach us a great deal in situations such as this.

> The Aikidoist takes the energy (attack) offered, blends his energy with it, avoids all resistance, and leads the attacker where he has no choice but to fall. Especially, the Aikidoist is adept at first avoiding, and then utilizing, all resistance that might be offered. It is his forte to be able to do this without being caught up, mentally or physically, in a "struggle."[8]

The concept of blending with an attacker enlightens the practice of "rolling with resistance." As we have seen, this approach of sidestepping resistance so that it is not faced directly is crucial because direct confrontation is likely to escalate resistance rather than reduce it.

> In Aikido blending, the energy of an opponent's attack is never resisted or rejected. The Aikidoist takes the mental position of welcoming the attack, both as an opportunity to restore harmony and as a chance to practice the art... The practitioner views resistance not as a problem one wishes would go away, but

---

[7] Erickson, *An Hypnotic Technique For Resistant Patients,* The American Journal Of Clinical Hypnosis, Volume 7, Number 1, July 1964.

[8] Rod Windle & Michael Samko (1992) *Hypnosis, Ericksonian Hypnotherapy, and Aikido*, American Journal of Clinical Hypnosis, 34:4, p. 263.

rather as essential "raw energy" that can lead to ultimate solutions.[9]

Strategies for working with resistance are most effective when they take advantage of the energy that has arisen within the interaction. By recognising, accepting and even honouring that resistance, it can then be redirected. We will discuss such strategies now, with the explicit caveat that we are more focused on the mindset involved than specific techniques to be employed.

1. Listening to Resistance

Perhaps our first response to encountering resistance in our interactions is to notice it and pay attention to it. Yapko writes that resistance can be viewed as a 'dynamic communication' which reveals limitations the client is currently experiencing. Encountering resistance can serve to encourage us to pay more attention to the client's experience, asking questions about the direction we are going in and the approach we are taking.

Are our clients comfortable with what we are asking them to do? Is it something they can currently get on board with, or are they not in the emotional or mental space to do so? Do they even understand what we are asking of them? Questions about the quality of our pre-talk and their levels of expectation are obviously relevant here.

Of course, resistance – being, as it is, an interactional phenomena – raises questions about our responses, as much as our client's. For example, we may notice the

---
9   Ibid, p. 267.

presence of frustration, or the urge to persuade, or confront our clients. These are a clear communication to us that we need to rethink our direction.

2. Go Slow

Listening to resistance likely involves a previous step of slowing down. Paying attention to our client's experience will almost certainly involve putting the breaks on. If resistance is in the air, then it is a safe bet that client and hypnotist are not on the same page. A common reason for this is because the hypnotist has shot-off on their own journey, with their own agenda, leaving the struggling client back in the chair.

The encouragement to slow down allows the client and hypnotist to get in sync again, but also provides an opportunity to consider the speed of progress. It may be that even after they are both back on the same page, the hypnotist may need to reconsider his expectations around the speed of travel.

Thinking of the analogy of a dance may be useful here. When we become aware of resistance, it is as if the hypnotist and/or client become aware that one of them is doing the waltz and the offer is performing a cha-cha. Slowing down enables the dancers to reconnect, but it may also serve to inform the hypnotist that they had selected a dance that was too difficult, or too quick for their client. After all, even if you are teaching an upbeat dance, you have to initially slow it down to do so.

3. Utilise

Whatever arises during the hypnotic interaction can be utilised. In one sense, all of these strategies are examples of utilisation. However, it can be even more specific than this.

As a rather obvious and inelegant example, if you have a client who is not responding well to suggestions for an arm levitation, you might redirect this as emphasising muscle relaxation and heaviness, or even stick their arm to their leg. If your client is struggling to narrow their focus in on one thing, or appears to have an over-active mind, you might ask them to pay attention to as many distractions as they possibly can, whilst simultaneously noticing every sensation that their body experiences. Some clients may not achieve the eye-lock experience commonly seen at the beginning of the Elman induction. In that case, you can redirect into an open-eyes (or 'waking trance') approach.

If you attempt to perform a Bandler Handshake induction and their hand refuses to stay up in front of their face, you might want to keep hold of the hand – or even invite them to intentionally hold it up – and turn your attention to their focus on that hand, beginning an eye-fixation.

Some clients might shuffle around more than the hypnotist would like. This shuffling can be encouraged to continue, until they find themselves getting gradually more comfortable. Or, you might even invite them to switch chairs and find which chair they can more easily sink into.

In fact, as with all of these points, this goes further than the induction. For example, during a therapy session, it may become apparent that your client seems to struggle with giving up control. Perhaps they were nervous that you were trying to control them when you began. Maybe they feel like their partner is trying to change them. So, you can utilise that and help them learn strategies for self-mastery, to take back control of their own life from all of the negative thought-patterns and behaviours that they want to overcome.

4. Go Indirect

If resistance seems to be an issue, you might want to consider being less direct. This is particularly the case if it feels as if the hypnotist and the client are not 'dancing' well together. If you are simply not on the same page, or feel like you are butting heads, a more indirect approach would be recommended.

A rather obvious example of using indirect language is the common experience of talking about head-lice. How many parents have been discussing the latest outbreak of lice at school only to find one of them compelled to scratch their heads, all without any explicit suggestions to do so? Similarly, rather than commanding or directly suggesting the experience or phenomena you are hoping for, you might talk about it in a metaphorical sense, or discuss someone else who experienced something similar.

Indirect suggestions can take place on the non-verbal level as well. Experienced hypnotherapists will know all too well that it is often possible to have your client take a deep breath without even mentioning it. You can merely shuffle a bit in your seat as you say, "And as you get yourself comfortable... you can..." then take a deep breath as you say, "relax whenever you're ready, in whichever way is most natural to you." You will very often find your client mirroring your behaviour, without explicitly being asked to, or being told that taking a deep breath is a good way to begin relaxing.

Another way to approach this is to raise the possibility of the behaviour, but not explicitly suggest it:

> "You do not need to pay attention to the degree that you relax further as you continue to breathe-in nice and easily…"

You may want to consider inductions that tend to feel less like the hypnotist is doing something to the client, or imposing his will on the client through the techniques he is performing on them. Inductions like *My Friend John*,[10] *The Fake Induction*,[11] *The Fractionation Conversation*[12] or *the Leisure Induction*[13] are all worthy of consideration.

Of course, the most natural way to be indirect may be to tell hypnotic stories. A great resource for this can be found within the world of Acceptance and Commitment Therapy, which makes good use of metaphor. You may also wish to acquaint yourself with books that share intentionally therapeutic stories. A number of these are included in the appendices.

5. Be Permissive

We will say more about this when discussing so-called

---

[10] http://www.howtodoinductions.com/inductions/mfj
[11] http://www.howtodoinductions.com/inductions/fake
[12] http://www.howtodoinductions.com/inductions/fractionation
[13] http://www.howtodoinductions.com/inductions/leisure

"polarity responders," but adopting a more permissive approach can be especially useful when facing resistance. Rather than saying something like, "And as that arm begins to rise into the air..." You might opt instead for language like, "And I wonder if you will begin to notice any changing sensations in that arm there. Some people find that their arm begins to feel lighter, or it may start feeling heavier and heavier, or it may even feel exactly the same..."

To build on this point, being less attached to specific outcomes and generally more open-ended is something that would serve many hypnotists well. The less invested that practitioners are in a specific outcome, the less likely they are to encounter resistance. Thus, "going with the flow" and utilising what our clients bring to the interaction are useful ways to proceed. *My Friend John* and *the Leisure Induction* are perfectly suited to such an approach as they are not taught as scripts to be followed, but a method of working interactively, taking what our clients give us and feeding that back to them.

6. Get Active

Many inductions involve the client sitting or standing somewhere, whilst the hypnotist does something to them. The client is essentially passive, almost a victim, if you will. If fear, issues of control, less than perfect motivation, or mismatched expectations are an issue, then such an approach is a disastrous way to proceed.

It is preferable to invite your client to work with you, to co-create the experience to come. So, give them something to do, something to get involved in. If nothing else, this helps them to shift focus from waiting for something to be done to them, to participating in its creation. Any induction that involves an interactive or participatory process is desirable. PHRIT would be but one example.[14]

7. Check Your Goals

If you encounter resistance, it is always a good idea to go back to the earlier stated goals for your session. What is it that your client wants to get out of the experience? Is your induction and general approach in line with that? Is it possible that your client perceives a conflict between their goal and what is taking place? For example, if they have stated that they want to get a handle on their anxiety, do they feel as though the induction is a stressful or anxiety-inducing event?

This works the other way around as well. Not only does the induction need to avoid contradicting the client's goals, but it is helpful if it is obvious how it works towards them.

8. Manage Expectations

Along with revisiting client goals goes the topic of managing expectations. What did your client think, if anything, was going to happen? Does the induction make sense to them as an aspect of that, or does it militate against their expectations?

We will look at this further when discussing so-called "analyticals," but it is worth raising the importance of

---

14 http://www.howtodoinductions.com/inductions/phrit

phenomena at this point. It is my opinion that most inductions should involve phenomena. However, is the phenomena in line with their expectations? Does it confirm and build upon what they were expecting? Or does it seem unrelated, unexpected or even contradictory to them?

Of course, some clients may have little expectation. It is important to meet them where they are. You do not want to choose an induction that feels, to them, out of their depth. There is nothing wrong with slowing down - even reversing things a little bit - and prolonging your pre-talk, or otherwise spending more time and attention on setting the scene. Alternatively, an induction that is a progressive experience might be appropriate, as it builds on the client's ongoing and increasing experience. This could include anything from a typical *Progressive Muscle Relaxation*[15] to something like the *Elman Induction*.[16]

Who is the Expert?

A number of the points above rely to a great deal on the hypnotist being willing to give up the expert position. There is an unfortunate tendency within hypnosis circles for hypnotists to believe their own hype and therefore to have – and often reflect – an elevated opinion of themselves. To a certain extent, this is understandable. Such hypnotists may have undertaken hundreds of hours of training, often receiving certification with titles such as "Master," or "Advanced." In reality, these mean next to nothing, but they are a frequent marketing approach,

---
15 http://www.howtodoinductions.com/inductions/pmr
16 http://www.howtodoinductions.com/inductions/elman

presumably intended to elicit confidence from clients.

On top of that, Stage Hypnosis and a rather old school approach to hypnotherapy puts much weight on the hypnotist's prowess and powerful persona. This is no doubt useful in some contexts and may still have its place in therapy, but it is one of the first things to reconsider if you are experiencing resistance.

You may well be a hypnotist with years of experience and countless testimonials celebrating your therapeutic expertise. However, you are not the expert *on your client*. They are. So, where resistance is experienced, put the brakes on, take a step back and listen to what your client is communicating.

Learn which directions they can and cannot go in, how quickly they can go and how they like to travel. Instead of adding to a situation where they are a passive recipient of your excellence, invite them to step-up as co-pilot of a progressive phenomenal learning experience. In my experience, you will encounter far less resistance with such an approach – either from you, your client, or the wonderful interaction of you both.

EXERCISE

What do you think about this concept of resistance?

Is it too optimistic, charitable, or naive?

How might it change the way you do inductions?

How might it change the way you relate to your clients?

How might it change the way you relate to others generally?

GRAHAM OLD

Mary, Mary, Quite Contrary

I am sure that many of us will have met people, whether family, friends, clients, or colleagues, who seem to almost instinctively disagree with anything and everything. It appears to be an automatic reaction for them to reject any proposition put to them and question every statement they hear, or at the very least, respond with, "Yes, but..." Within the world of NLP, such people are often known as 'polarity responders.'

To be honest, I am not sure that I believe in the existence of polarity responders, any more than I believe in resistance or analyticals. That is, the people that such words refer to may well exist, but I am not sure that the labels are the most useful way to view them.

Here is how I think of it: much of my work with clients is intended to help introduce some psychological flexibility into their lives. One of the ways that we can start to do this is to sow seeds that question some of the static characterisations that people make of themselves. For example, as long as someone sees themselves as a blusher, you may have an unnecessarily hard time getting beyond that. They are seeing it as an aspect of their identity. In their mind, it is who they are. Things become notably easier if they can see that blushing is something that they do, not who they are.

After all, very few of us go through our entire lives without changing significant aspects of our characters, or adjusting our model of the world. Do we really want to teach our clients – or those being trained to work with their own clients – that people are defined by how they are seen during one snapshot of their lives?

So, am I suggesting that the people I alluded to in this chapter's opening paragraph do not exist? No, not at all. However, I am questioning whether we ever really know enough about someone, or their thought patterns, to give them such static labels. Recently, I was reading an article by an NLP trainer who even said that such contrary behaviour was "hard-wired" in the polarity responder. Not only is there zero scientific evidence for such a claim, but I would posit that it is therapeutically irresponsible to box people in with such unmovable statements.

Whilst I fully accept that we all face polarity responses from people in all the various spheres of our lives, I do not think it is useful to label people "polarity responders." The exception to this may be if the person using such terminology is using it very loosely to simply refer to someone currently responding in such a way.

Why do we See Polarity Responses?

There are all manner of reasons why someone might demonstrate polarity responses. Someone who is insecure or immature may see such behaviour as a way to prove you wrong and demonstrate how smart they are. Alternatively, someone more mature or insightful may genuinely think they are being helpful.

However, we can probably categorise a number of

reasons for polarity responses, recognising that this in no way captures the complexity of reasons for human behaviour.

Fear is a fairly frequent motivation behind automatic contradictory responses. Someone who does not feel safe, or secure within themselves, may act in such a manner as a defensive strategy.

Learned thought patterns are a common reason for such behaviour. For whatever reason, someone learns to act in such a way until it becomes essentially automatic. These are usually the people that we are told are "hard-wired" to respond as they do.

Above-average intelligence may be a factor in some cases. As we said above, in someone with less self-awareness, they may view the behaviour as a way to show their superior intelligence. However, for others it may be that they simply notice more than the average person, seeing the flaws or holes in our arguments and plans. I will say a little more about this below, but I believe that those who frequently offer polarity responses are often skilled at noticing exceptions and inconsistencies - including exceptions to the rule – and seeing fine details that others may miss.

This last point reminds us to consider that *we* may be the cause of the polarity response. Are we really so assured of our own opinions and actions that any time someone disagrees, or sees a problem with them, we conclude there is something wrong with them? Much of the literature on this topic would suggest the answer might be, Yes! It is not difficult to find writings that speak of "handling polarity responders," or, "dealing with difficult clients," as if such people are naughty children who have stepped out of line. Is it not perfectly feasible that the reason we are provoking polarity responses is because what we are saying is illogical, irrational, incorrect, or simply foolish? At the very least, we should consider that it may seem that way to our clients.

All of these reasons can be amplified by our way of being with our clients. Much as we suggested resistance may be better viewed as an interactional occurrence, polarity responses do not exist in a vacuum. Are we presenting ourselves in an overbearing way, that provokes a client to put their defences up? Do we project an expert persona, inviting someone to prove us wrong? Is it possible that we respond with our own polarity responses, thus initiating a tug-of-war with our clients?

Working with Polarity Responses

Unsurprisingly, much of the advice that follows repeats ideas first suggested in the chapter on Responding to Resistance.

1. Invite Open-Ended Responses

This is perhaps the first step in giving up the expert position. Instead of conveying the idea that we are to be obeyed at all costs – thus inviting rebellion in some people – we can invite people to respond in any number of ways. Therapists need to learn that their agenda is not the only one on the table. For some people, their sense of freedom or control may far outweigh their inclination to obey us, or their desire to break-free from the issue they visit us to resolve.

HYPNOSIS WITH THE HARD TO HYPNOTISE

One way to make slightly open-ended responses is to make use of double-binds. An example might be:

> "As you relax even further, you may go deeper into trance in a few seconds, or perhaps in a minute or two."

This makes use of 'free choice among comparable alternatives.' This seems to be a preferable description than the more common, 'double-bind,' or illusion of choice.[17] Nevertheless, it is not a genuinely open-ended suggestion and is likely not as clever or clandestine as therapists might like to think.

A fully open-ended suggestion would sound more like:

> "Shortly your right hand, or it may be your left hand, will begin to lift up, or it may press down, or it may not move at all, but we will just wait to see just what happens. Maybe the thumb will be first, or you may feel something happening in your little finger, but the really important thing is not whether your hand lifts up or presses down, or just remains still; rather, it is your ability to sense fully whatever feelings may develop in your hand."[18]

Even within that example, you might notice a spectrum of "openness." Although the initial suggestion is completely open-ended, the next suggestion ('Maybe the thumb will be first, or you may feel something happening

---

17 See *Creative Choice in Hypnosis*, edited by Rossi and Ryan.
18 Erickson, quoted in Rubin Battino, *Ericksonian Approaches*, p.139.

in your little finger') at least implies that some movement is to be expected. This is then followed by another fully open suggestion, acknowledging that perhaps nothing will happen. Finally, this is tied-in to a therapeutic suggestion of kinaesthetic awareness and focus.

For some hypnotists, this may be a completely alien way to work. For others, it may be more familiar, but unexpected within the induction. I would suggest that the ability to work in this way is an extremely useful skill to develop. It is especially useful for those situations where it may appear as if someone is reacting to our attempts to impose our will on them.

2. Use permissive language

This is an element of the previous point and something we addressed when looking at resistance. However, it may bear a little further exploration at this point. Any time you feel like there is an element of conflict or confrontation within your interactions – regardless of where it is coming from – it is worth considering if you could be more permissive, inviting or participatory.

As well as *being* permissive (as seen above), it helps to use explicitly permissive language. So, you may want to avoid saying things like:

> "As you close your eyes, you will go further into that relaxation."

Instead, you might want to say:

> "I don't know if you will go further into that

relaxation when you close your eyes..."

Words and phrases that are worth having on the tip of your tongue include:

"Maybe"
"Perhaps"
"I wonder..."
"You could..."
"You might..."
"...or not."
"I don't know..."
"Some people may..."
"I'm curious to know if..."

3. Give them something to disagree with!

Although the previous two points functioned to not give your client something to argue against, this one does the opposite. If your client seems inclined, for whatever reason, to respond in a contrary manner, why not use this to their advantage?

To repeat one of the indirect suggestions we gave in the last chapter:

"You do not need to pay attention to the degree that you relax further as you continue to breathe-in nice and easily..."

However, you can go much further in terms of provoking a polarity response. For example, instead of inviting eye-closure, you could say something like, "you do not need to pay any attention to the tiredness in your eyelids." That is an almost guaranteed way to have them focus on the increasing heaviness in their eyes.

Other simple examples might include:

"You will probably disagree, but…"

"I suspect this is not something you'd like to take part in…"

"I have an idea that I think you're not going to like, but I wanted to see what you think anyway."

"You probably don't want to close your eyes."

Effectively, you are inviting them to respond to your negativity, which they are inclined to do with an opposite response. Of course, the opposite response to a negative is a positive!

Another way to achieve the same end is to return to our earlier examples of open-ended suggestions. However, this time you will want to give the impression that one of the outcomes is less likely to be chosen then the other.

This would look something like:

"As you relax even further, you may go deeper

into trance in a few seconds, or perhaps in a minute or two, or even as soon as you close your eyes..."

We can see how this might work with Erickson's open-ended suggestion for arm-levitation that we quoted earlier:

"Shortly your right hand, or it may be your left hand, will begin to lift up, or it may press down, or it may not move at all, but we will just wait to see just what happens."

When polarity responses are at play, presenting a choice as unlikely, or unexpected, is essentially the same as saying, "You probably won't do this, but..." In this example, depending on what intonation is employed, the lack of movement is the option most likely to be selected.

Utilisation! Utilisation! Utilisation!

The three strategies above are all examples of utilisation. They are ways to listen to your client, respect their behaviour and work with what they give you. You don't rebuke the polarity responses, seek to overcome them, or label your client because of them. Instead, you honour them.

I wrote above that many of those who frequently offer polarity responses are adept at noticing exceptions and seeing details that others may miss. This is a skill to be encouraged and built upon.

If you work against these kind of responses, you may inadvertently give your client the message that they are broken in some way. Moreover, you discourage them from developing a skill that may actually be therapeutically beneficial.

Rather, if you are working with someone who is prone to spot exceptions and notice glitches in a pattern, or highlight the inconsistencies of certain thoughts and behaviours, recognise that they are in a prime position to co-create their own therapeutic solutions. They can be encouraged to think outside of the box, see possibilities that are not even considered by others and become aware of times when their apparently entrenched and unceasing problem was not present.

EXERCISE

Have you encountered "Polarity Responders," either in life, or in your hypnosis practice?

How do you respond when faced with polarity responses?

Is there anything you would now do differently based on this chapter?

Are there any contexts where *you* might be considered a polarity responder?

GRAHAM OLD

The Auto Dual Induction Transcript

It is not clear who first developed the Auto Dual Induction, though in some ways it is a variation of a number of others (for example, My Friend John).[19]

The induction is commonly associated with John Kappas of the Hypnosis Motivational Institute. Kappas taught that the Induction was most effective for clients that were "intellectually suggestible," yet resistant.

I do not necessarily classify clients in the same way as Kappas. However, I do share his enthusiasm for this induction. In short, this involves having the client repeat suggestions to themselves. The theory is that this bypasses any resistance they may feel, as they do not experience themselves being hypnotised by someone else, so they have nothing to resist.

In some ways, this induction may appear to contradict the strategies suggested in the previous two chapters. After all, it can come across as very direct. However, closer examination will show that whilst the language may be direct, the induction as a whole is indirect. I would invite you to consider other ways that this induction employs the strategies discussed above, albeit in a more covert way.

---

[19] The chapter 'Actively Participating in Hypnosis' in my earlier book *My Friend John* shares some examples that incorporate this technique.

H(ypnotist): "Okay, let's do something a little bit different."

C(lient): "Okay."

H: "What we are going to do today is, I am going to invite you to hypnotise yourself. How does that sound?"

C: "Er, okay."

H: "So, let's start by having you place your feet flat on the floor. And I would like you to find somewhere to look at on this wall here... perhaps the corner of the picture, or that spot on the wall there where the reflection is creating a small rainbow.

"Now, let your eyes rest on that... and just look at that point... just keep focusing on that spot, without moving your eyes...

"And I am going to give you instructions to pass on to yourself. So, in a way, you are my assistant hypnotist repeating the instructions, as well as the client receiving them. Okay?"

C: "Okay."

HYPNOSIS WITH THE HARD TO HYPNOTISE

H: "What I would like you to do now is repeat my words after me. And you can stop when you hear me say, "Zero... Deep asleep now." At that point, you can just let go and go inside. So, repeat after me...

"I am preparing to enter a state of hypnosis..."

C: "I am preparing to enter a state of hypnosis..."

H: "I will count down from five to zero and with each count I will become more deeply relaxed."

C: "I will count down from five to zero and with each count I will become more deeply relaxed."

H: "When I reach zero, I will go into a deep hypnotic sleep."[20]

C: "When I reach zero, I will go into a deep hypnotic sleep."

H: "Five... My breathing is deep, gentle and rhythmic."

---

20 It is presumed that any time you use the idea of sleep, you have explained to your clients that this is not the same as literal physical sleep.

C: "Five... My breathing is deep, gentle and rhythmic."

H: "Four... I begin to feel heaviness in my eyelids, as I become drowsier and sleepier."

C: "Four... I begin to feel heaviness in my eyelids, as I become drowsier and sleepier."

H: "Three... I begin to feel every muscle, nerve and fibre in my body relaxing, deeply relaxing."

C: "Three... I begin to feel every muscle, nerve and fibre in my body relaxing, deeply relaxing."

H: "Two... My arms, my legs, my entire body is now deeply relaxed."

C: "Two... My arms, my legs, my entire body is now deeply relaxed."

H: "One... My eyelids grow even heavier, breathing becoming more rhythmic. I am deeply relaxed."

C: "One... My eyelids grow even heavier, breathing becoming more rhythmic. I am deeply relaxed."

HYPNOSIS WITH THE HARD TO HYPNOTISE

H: "Zero... deep asleep now."

EXERCISE

Practice the Auto Dual Induction.

Are there other inductions into which you could incorporate elements of auto dual?

What are the benefits on an auto dual approach?

Are there any downsides to this approach to the induction?

HYPNOSIS WITH THE HARD TO HYPNOTISE

The Myth of the Analytical Subject

One of the most feared circumstances for many beginning hypnotherapists is encountering a so-called 'analytical.' These intellectual bullies are the scourge of the world of hypnosis and rightly shied away from. Thankfully, they are also completely imaginary.

I am not denying that there are some people who are routinely more analytical than the average person. Neither am I questioning that you may encounter some clients who naturally want to analyse and dissect everything that you are doing. The thing I am questioning is the existence of cerebral bogey-men who are out to withstand any foolish hypnotist who thinks they can hypnotise them, because their brains are always working on full throttle and almost impossible to over-power.

"Analyticals"

At the risk of sounding as if I am simply being pedantic, I would like to begin a rather lengthy diversion and challenge the whole language around "analyticals." My position is that such language is lazy, presumptuous and limiting. At best, it classifies someone according to one aspect of their being. At worst, it denies another human being's individuality and often writes them off as beyond our help.

I myself would be classed as "an analytical" by many people. I would object strongly. For, although my thinking-style is prone towards analysis and detailed examination, I can not be summed-up by this one word. Even if we focus solely on the moment of induction, I can also be emotional, curious, enthusiastic and more. However, even if I was solely analytical at the point of induction – which I would suggest is impossible, given the complexity of human thought and behaviour – to therefore label me "an analytical" makes a static and rigid categorisation out of a dynamic and contextual trait. After all, are not most of us analytical in some contexts?

Additionally, it is simply not the case that everyone who is labelled as "analytical" is in fact an analytical thinker. Unfortunately, some hypnotists lazily – and, let's face it, dismissively – apply the term to anyone that they find it difficult to hypnotise. However, this involves a number of unhelpful assumptions.

Firstly, it assumes that the 'fault' for the 'failure' to go into hypnosis lies with the client. The hypnotist does what they usually do to hypnotise someone, and when that does not work they presume that their client is doing something wrong. The hypnotist may be convinced that they gave a perfect pre-talk and that they are working with a willing and fear-free subject. Therefore, they presume, the client is resisting at the subconscious level, probably by analysing everything and not just going along with the process. This whole evaluation says far more about the hypnotist's frustration and lack of flexibility than the client's mind.

Secondly, such an assessment assumes that because

the client is listening and thinking about everything that is said to them – but still not "going under" - then they are actually *over*-thinking what is taking place. Some hypnotists will rightly later question their client on their experience and will learn that the subject heard every word, considered them carefully and thought about what was taking place. Some of these hypnotists then conclude that the issue is that the client is thinking too much and getting preoccupied with that, rather than simply giving-in to the experience. They then assume that the client is one of the dreaded "analyticals" they had been warned about and their confidence drains away.

The interesting thing about this second assumption is that there is no evidence the client is over-thinking anything. After all, who is to say how much thinking is too much? What actually constitutes over-thinking, in contrast to simply thinking? It would seem that the real issue is that the client goes on evaluating what is taking place beyond the point at which the hypnotist had hoped they would be "under." (It might be noted here that the whole concept of clients being "under" and somehow then less thoughtful, with their conscious mind asleep and their subconscious mind unthinkingly responding to suggestion is a little outdated and not at all in line with contemporary hypnosis research.)

Imagine for a moment, interviewing 100 people who had not responded to an induction and asking them "What were you doing during the induction?" My suspicion is that close to 100 of them would answer that they were listening and thinking. That is, after all, what they are supposed to be doing! However, the frustrated hypnotist hears this and concludes that the problem is that they were listening too well and thinking too much. The hypnotist assumes that they were over-thinking and that this in some way hindered their responses. In short, they carried on thinking, after the hypnotist had reached the point where they thought the thinking would stop.

Thus is born the idea that over-thinking or being analytical is the enemy of hypnosis. And that is then applied further with the assumption that anyone who is difficult to hypnotise is therefore an analytical.

Of course, some people *are* more analytical in their thinking – for all manner of reasons. They like to analyse, examine, reason, and can be suspicious of anything that they cannot logically explain. We do them a great disservice as hypnotists if we continue to propagate the idea that they are difficult to hypnotise. That merely quashes both their expectation and the confidence of the person hypnotising them. Instead, it seems to me that we simply need to learn new ways to work with their powerful mind.

Hypnotic Thinking

As we have noted previously, there are a number of reasons why someone may be difficult to hypnotise. It is a rather drastic mistake to presume that someone is an analytical thinker, or resistant, whenever we encounter such situations. Even if we consider an extremely narrow set of circumstances, such as the client's thinking during the induction, there are all sorts of reasons that may be an issue. They may have had a difficult day, which has put them in a particularly pessimistic mood. They may be suffering from clinical depression. They may be too desperate, anxious, or invested in what is taking place and interfere with the process by attempting to assist the hypnotist. They may struggle to get absorbed in cognitive experiences. They may be intoxicated. They may be out of practice with using their imagination. They may not believe that anything good could happen to them. They may be suffering with auditory hallucinations, or intrusive thoughts. They may be over-medicated. They may not like you.

If we look at all of this thinking – whether that involves thinking styles, personality types, learned behaviours, or circumstantial reactions – the one thing they have in common is that they appear to miss the cues that the hypnotist offers during the induction process. In short, the client's mind is not doing what the hypnotist needs it to be doing to go into hypnosis.[21] This may be because the client is caught in some kind of cognitive loop already (such as, "this won't work for me; I'm useless!"), or it may be because the client does not intuit what is required of them.

With some clients, you can talk indirectly about sensations of lightness and their arm will begin to rise. With others, you might describe what an arm levitation feels like, or describe someone else experiencing one, and they begin to respond in kind. However, other clients will look at you completely unaware that the unspoken intention is for them to begin experiencing this themselves. This is why, for example, someone might respond very well to the heavy book / helium balloons suggestibility test, but completely 'fail' at arm levitation

---

21 At least, it is not doing it in a way that aligns with the way that the hypnotist is currently attempting to work!

as a phenomena during the formal hypnosis. They were completely unaware it applied to them in the same way!

Clients like this are just not thinking in a hypnotic way. This could be because they may not naturally be very imaginative or kinaesthetic thinkers. Or, they may not intuitively 'get' hypnosis. Or due to one hundred and one things taking place in their life, they may be over-focused on other thoughts and feelings at the point we are trying to hypnotise them. They are not inclined to automatically respond emotionally or kinaesthetically to what the hypnotist is saying.

It may be possible to change someone who is not naturally a hypnotic thinker, or currently thinking in an hypnotic way. However, I would rather change what I was doing, so that the way they are thinking is precisely the way I need them to be in order to go into hypnosis! That is, rather than change their mind to make it fit my pre-defined approach, I will change my method to fit their mind. At the very least, I would suggest that this should be our first tactic.

The following pointers are worth bearing in mind when working in this way.

Can I Borrow Your Trance?

The irony with all of this, is that even if the client is prone to being analytical, that is no hindrance to hypnosis. I know that I am not the only hypnotist who has found that some of their best responders ever were students completing a doctorate, or University professors.

Let's face it, everyone can be "analytical." We all like to take-in what is happening around us and notice what is happening to us, evaluating and making sense of it. We may vary in the degree to which we do this, but all things being equal we all do it at times. The thing that is different about those thinkers formerly known as 'analyticals' is that they get *absorbed* in their analysis. This is something for hypnotists to welcome and even celebrate. It is certainly not something to fear or work against!

Back when I believed in the myth of the analytical subject, I used to say that analyticals are permanently in a state of trance. I would still say that there is some truth in this, even if I may now choose to speak of people a little more holistically and respectfully. It still seems to me that there is a sense in which some people are so habitually prone towards analysis that they could be said to be in a trance at such times. So, in some situations, a hypnotist may be trying to induce a hypnotic trance in an 'analytical,' completely oblivious to the fact that they are already in trance! Some conceptions of hypnosis view it as occurring when the mind is locked-in on one idea.[22] Yet, an argument could be made that you have trance the moment a client is locked-in on the very act of thinking. It is not the thought of one idea that they are focusing on, but the singular experience of thinking itself.

If this idea has merit, then it may be that the task of a hypnotist at such moments is not so much inducing hypnosis, but of managing trance. Simply redirecting what is already taking place, rather than seeking to create something new, is what is required. It seems likely that another consequence of this idea is that the

---

[22] James Braid, the man who coined the term "hypnosis", later attempted to change it to "monoideism." meaning focus on one idea.

hypnotist does not need to work to stop the client from thinking. Instead, he only needs to give the client something else to think about, or teach them how to think in a different way.

This idea that some analytically-inclined thinkers may be more familiar with trance than we assume strikes me as a significant one. We will apply it further later in the chapter.

Think, Think and Think Some More

You have probably encountered people who wrongly believed that the hypnotic experience was akin to being dead. They expected complete unconsciousness, not hearing a single sound, or being aware of the experience in any way. It has to be said that some people do have that sort of experience, though even in those cases it often fluctuates up and down, in and out, rather than being fully awake at one minute and then completely out of it the next.

However, it seems that the majority of people do not experience hypnosis in that way at all. They may continue to be aware of their surroundings throughout the entire process, even if they find their focus to be fixed on your words. This is especially true for so-called analyticals. This is one of the reasons that I rely on phenomena, as will be explained below. Such thinkers continue to think all the way through the induction, sometimes causing both them and their hypnotist to conclude that they had not been hypnotised.

Yet, if we start from the understanding that many people do not experience hypnosis as a non-thinking state, then this is less of a problem. And if we accept that some thinkers will most likely continue to think all of the way through, regardless of what we do, we can begin to use this to their good. I tell such clients, "You will probably continue to think all through the process and I encourage you to do that." In that way, when they notice that they are thinking, it does not become a sign that they are not under hypnosis, as I told them that was likely to happen. However, it is *how* they are thinking that I encourage them to consider.

I use the example of seeing a film at the cinema. Obviously, we do not stop thinking during a film, even a good film. In fact, it could be said that we think more attentively than we usually do. We focus so much on what is taking place that it can even elicit emotional reactions from us, as if part of us has accepted that for the next two hours what we are seeing on the screen is our new reality. I then reveal that I am a bit of a movie geek. I love films, almost everything about them. I enjoy considering the influences on the director, noticing parts that were inspired by other films, techniques that were borrowed from others and so on. Yet, I ask my client, what would happen if I only thought like that throughout the whole film? Most people respond by telling me that I would not fully enjoy the film. And they are right! I could still enjoy it on one level, but I would not *experience* the film. Ironically, for all of my interest in the mechanics behind the film, I end up not seeing the film as the director intended.

I then suggest that if I spent the whole movie thinking, *"Am I enjoying this? Am I really experiencing the film as the film-maker intended? Am I spectating well?"* I would not be allowing myself to really get into the film. All of my focus on worrying about whether I was doing 'spectating' properly would become the very thing that lessened my enjoyment of the film. By this point, most of my clients are ahead of me, but I like to make sure the lesson has been heard.

I tell them that I don't want them to worry about the fact that they are thinking. I reiterate that they will be thinking all of the way through. And I explicitly encourage them to do that. I add that I want them to think about every single thing that I say and that they experience. In fact, the only thing I might encourage them not to think about *too much* is the fact that they are thinking! Doing that would be like going to the cinema and spending the whole time asking yourself if you were enjoying the film. Just enjoy the film!

> "Think and think and think some more," I say. "And let's use that powerful mind of yours, to discover some of those changes you could be making."

Of course, what I have done here is effectively told the client, "just go with it!" Yet, I have done so in a way that respects the kind of mind they have. Therefore, they will not feel threatened to engage with the experience, knowing that they can actually use their mind to do so, without worrying about whether it has switched-off enough.

HYPNOSIS WITH THE HARD TO HYPNOTISE

Say What You Want!

Some of those who are not inclined to hypnotic thinking do naturally think in an analytical or critical way. One thing that such thinkers often do during an induction is critically assess what the hypnotist is saying. They consider if it makes sense to them and ultimately what it means. They may evaluate the meaning of everything they hear. Consequently, hypnotists need to consider carefully what they are saying.

Bearing this in mind, I am somewhat troubled by the common assertion that the best way to work with "an analytical" is to either confuse of shock them. I will say in a later chapter why I do not use confusion in such a way, but I am not convinced that shock is the answer either. The assumption seems to be that you have to shock analyticals into hypnosis, because if you use any other kind of induction, they will think about what you're saying. Have you ever thought about how ridiculous that sounds? Of course, they will think about what you're saying. That's what they do! And if what you are saying is not getting the job done, maybe you need to reconsider how and what you are saying – not just pummel your client into unconsciousness!

Of course, a reliance on shock inductions at such a time betrays a certain magical type of thinking. It seems to depend upon – or, at the very least, perpetuates – the idea that hypnosis is a "knocked-out" state involving a complete lack of awareness and consciousness. However, as stated above, that is simply not how most people experience hypnosis. In actual fact, it is the misconception that hypnotic trance always involves a blissful unconsciousness that is one of the main reasons that analytical thinkers may question if they were hypnotised. Additionally, this kind of approach often acts as if "sleep" is a magic word that is somehow hard-wired into our brains, such that saying it will drop someone automatically into a hypnotic trance.

This is not to say that shock inductions can not work in situations where you have been struggling to hypnotise someone. However, my belief is that usually in such cases, the successful hypnotee was not an 'analytical' in any accurate sense of the word. They may simply be someone who had a very high expectation that "sleep" produced the desired result, due to the representations of hypnosis in movies, or seeing a Stage Hypnotist at work. If someone responds so well to a shock induction, I do not see any way in which they can be classed as 'hard to hypnotise' or analytical.[23] If they are not thinking in a very hypnotic way, they will not be more likely to do so just because someone shocks them!

This has been a rather long-winded way to say that when you are working with an analytical-thinker, you should say what you mean. If you want your client to adopt a sleep-like posture, tell them to close their eyes and relax their shoulders. You can even invite them to let their mind begin to day-dream whenever it is ready. Do not just yell, "Sleep!" at them and expect the same result!

As a further example, do not presume that by simply telling someone that they are nice and relaxed that they are actually anything of the sort. Neither can you assume

---

23 Even if such an approach did work with analyticals, it is not a particularly therapeutic method, nor does it respect their way of being or unique gifts.

that by just inviting your client to relax that they will do so. For some people, even describing a state of relaxation or a relaxing scene will not be enough. You may need to explicitly tell them what to do.

> "And as you *picture that scene*, you can *begin to imagine* what it would feel like to be there... And allow yourself to begin to *experience that now...*"

You might then need to carry on explicitly inviting them to relax different parts of their bodies, whilst also noticing as the relaxation increases. Unless they eventually learn how to, they are unlikely to do this automatically. That's just not how they think.

Set the Right Expectations at the Start!

As with anyone, expectation plays an important role when working with analytical-thinkers, or anyone not thinking in an hypnotic way. So, it is important to set the right expectations from the beginning.

I like to include phenomena throughout my pre-talk. If I am mentioning seeing a movie – which I recommend as an extremely rich metaphor which can be taken in any number of directions – I will mention how just the right music can cause the hairs on your neck to stand, or goose-bumps to raise-up on your arms. As I mention this, I might rub my arms and shiver almost imperceptibly. I am seeding the idea that it is a natural reaction to have a physical response to something we merely think about. (Do not be afraid to get animated and act a little!)

Similarly, if I mention how even imagining biting into a lemon can set our teeth on edge, I will not expect my client to take my word for this. That would be to presume a more hypnotic and engaged style of thinking. Instead, I will have them actively imagine doing so, using it as a skill-building exercise, if necessary. This makes explicit and experiential the idea from the movie metaphor.

Then, I will often move on to using magnetic hands.[24] However, I do this as more than a mere convincer. Over the years, my use of this exercise has developed into an open-ended experience. I do not tell the client that their hands will move together, as I might do if I was using it as an induction. Admittedly, I talk about magnets, which obviously at least implies the hands *might* come together. Additionally, whilst I am positioning their hands, I may move them ever so slightly in and out, implying movement. Nevertheless, after I have set things up, I will ask them to focus on the spot between their hands, "the centre of the magnetic field," ask them to close their eyes and then say something like, "And let's see what happens."

Over the next few minutes, I may add encouragements to focus on the spot between their hands, "whilst feeling those magnets in your palms." Every now and again, I might say something like, "As you focus on that spot, allow yourself and your hands to *experience what it would feel like* when there are large magnets on the palms of your hands... So, all you need to do is *focus on that space between your hands*, whilst your hands *experience the feeling of those magnets...*"

The reason why I say that I now approach this as an

---

24 See http://www.howtodoinductions.com/exercises/magnetic

open-ended exercise is because there really is no pass or fail. I do not use this exercise to "convince" a client of anything. As it happens, I do not need or require their hands to come together. Instead, after we have finished, I ask them to talk me through everything they experienced, from the moment I touched their palms and placed the magnets there.

As you will know if you have used this exercise much, you can encounter a wide variety of responses. Experiences vary from hands coming together quickly and conclusively, to moving slowly and incompletely, to hardly any movement but some other experiential response (e.g. feeling "spaced-out" or super-focused), to no apparent response at all. Having said that, zero response of any kind is quite rare, as long as things were set-up well and the client felt free to experience whatever happens. Nevertheless, regardless of how the client describes their response, I will say to them, "that is quite possibly what hypnosis will feel like for you, the first time."

This statement usually conveys the idea that something "hypnotic" can take place even whilst the client feels completely normal. That is, no matter how "trancey" the client feels – spaced-out, focused, completely normal, or otherwise – they can still experience hypnosis taking place. This is important because, as we have stated, people who lean towards analytical thinking are usually very familiar with trance. We will expand on this below.

Less Focus on Trance

When I am working with so-called analyticals, I put next to no emphasis on trance. That is not to say that I do not emphasise phenomena or experience – quite the opposite, in fact – but I do not presume or dictate that my client will feel "under" in any way.

Think of it this way, if you are routinely in trance, it is not going to feel particularly exceptional to go to the same place, but by a different route. To the clients formerly known as analytical, trance will often feel completely unremarkable. The chances are – and how they responded to magnetic hands will be a good indicator of this – they will experience it as not much more than sitting there with their eyes closed.

So, my usual practice is to work with practically zero focus on trance. I consider it – or, rather the conscious experience of it – to be irrelevant. After all, I have already told them that the main thing to do is just watch and enjoy the film (i.e experience what happens), not to constantly wonder if they are watching the film and whether or not they are doing so properly.

This may involve using non-trance-based phenomena more than you have been doing. I would include under this classification, things like i) the Chevreul pendulum, ii) Bob Burn's *The Swan*, iii) a number of non-trance hypnosis effects, similar to those used by the likes of the Amazing Kreskin, iv) as well as ideomotor responses.

If you are not used to working in this way, it is worth acquainting yourself with the various principles and techniques involved. However, I would encourage you to avoid being taken-in by the mindset that sees this as something new, or advanced. If you have ever used any kind of suggestibility test, you have achieved non-trance-based hypnosis. In fact, I would go so far as to argue that if you have ever seen any kind of movement with the

Chevreul Pendulum, then you have more than likely experienced subconscious communication, which for our purposes is a quick and unscientific way of saying you have achieved hypnosis!

Active Experiences

In the days when I would still speak of resistant clients and analytical subjects, I used a phrase that I still refer to from time to time:

> Give the resistant client something to *do*.
> Give the analytical client something to *learn*.

To some degree, I still stand by that advice, though I would clearly word things differently. However, I would blow wide-open the client-base that I applied that advice to. I am now more likely to encourage all people to view their inductions as active learning experiences. That is, give your clients something to do *and* learn.

Whether your client routinely thinks in an analytical way, or does not think hypnotically for some other reason, it is almost always a good idea to use an active induction. After all, they have an active mind, so why not use it?

So, wherever possible, I like to get my clients involved in the induction process. A good example of the kind of thing I mean is the Fake Induction.[25] Not only is it interactive, which I always enjoy, but it also involves the client as an active participant in their hypnotic

---
25 See http://www.howtodoinductions.com/inductions/fake

experience.

Another example might be the PHRIT (Post-Hypnotic Re-induction Training) induction, which I have written about elsewhere.[26] This can be thought of as a fractionation process, where the client learns how to take themselves into and out of hypnosis, effectively going "deeper" with each re-entry.

Learning Experiences

There is a very significant reason why we suggest using an induction that is an active learning experience - and it goes to the heart of our approach to working with those we might find difficult to hypnotise. The key to our whole approach, as you will see time and time again, is utilisation.

As I said earlier in this chapter, when working with non-hypnotic thinkers - be they analytical or otherwise - I aim to adapt my method to their mind, not the other way round. You can see that approach reflected in nearly every point recommended in this section.

The clients we are considering tend to have active and alert minds, on the look out to understand everything they hear and experience. Seen from a different perspective, these clients may be seen as not merely analytical, but curious. They are eagerly paying attention to what is taking place, seeking to make sense of it and understand what is happening to them.

Rather than possessing a resistant, obstructive or oppositional mind, our clients can be thought of as almost like a young child, hungry for knowledge. Sure, it can be

---

[26] G. Old. (2014). *Revisiting Hypnosis*. Milton Keynes: Plastic Spoon.

frustrating as a parent trying to cook dinner, or driving on a busy road, to experience a child repeating, "Why? Why? Why?" seemingly without end. Yet, all parents know that it is a necessary and important stage in their child's growth. They are simply using their brain as they have to at that point in their life. And, the annoying repetition aside, it's the kind of thing that parents can look back on and smile with fondness.

None of this is to suggest that analytical thinkers are somehow immature, or emotionally stunted in some way. Instead, they can be thought of as managing to retain that childhood thirst for knowledge that many of us unfortunately lose as we get older. Their brains have kept hold of that inquisitiveness and if we hope to take them with us on a hypnotic journey, it is strongly advised to use inductions that meet their curiosity. Let them actively engage with the induction. And let them learn.

Progressive Inductions

Having mentioned the PHRIT induction, I should say some more about using progressive inductions.

In the past, I have performed shock inductions on so-called analyticals. And sometimes they appeared to be "zapped" just as effectively as anyone else. Yet, later discussion revealed that the experience had been no different to any other induction for them. They were still painfully aware that they were fully aware of everything happening to and around them. This puzzled me, so I pulled out all of the stops, using all of my sure-fire inductions, that never failed to work on other people. And, still, the feedback was almost always the same.

In fact, if anything, my analytical clients were less impressed by shock inductions than the other inductions that I had decided had failed. It seems that being fully aware of what was supposed to happen with something so dramatic, they had played along half-hoping that the experience of hypnosis would be as dramatic as the induction. When it was not, because as we have noted they usually experience trance in a fairly every-day way, there was even more disappointment and implied failure than usual.

In line with the advice to employ an induction that is an active learning experience, I would suggest using one that develops progressively. I am not necessarily thinking of a Progressive Muscle Relaxation here. However, the process as originally taught by Jacobsen (in contrast to the more common shortened form often used as an hypnotic induction) does provide valuable lessons in muscle tension and relaxation. Nevertheless, I am thinking more generally of any induction which functions as an educational process through which the client learns about using their mind in ways which promote hypnotic experiences.

A superb example of the sort of thing I have in mind is the Elman induction, of which I have written elsewhere in this series.[27] This can function as a process for clients to partake in, not simply a passive experience that is unleashed upon them. The client begins with the simple phenomena of catalepsy of a group of small muscles. In most versions of the induction, this is the eyelids and it has the effect of bypassing the client's critical faculty.[28] It

---

27 G. Old. (2014). *The Elman Induction*. Milton Keynes: Plastic Spoon.
28 I am here using the language of Elman to explain his induction, without

then progresses with a developing sense of both physical and mental relaxation, helped by fractionation. Along the way, the client experiences catalepsy of a large group of muscles – usually experienced as an arm-drop – and then eventually amnesia by suggestion.

The Elman induction can be framed and presented in a number of ways. If you view it in an Elmanian way, you might want to teach it as a means of going into deeper and deeper states of hypnosis. However, that is by no means the only way to explain the process. It can also be thought of as a progressive experience of selective thinking and an introduction to an increasing number of hypnotic phenomena.

It is my belief that there are few teaching tools as effective as the Elman induction, for clients who are analytical. Understood correctly, it is a powerful and efficient process that all hypnotists should be aware of.

Stop Trying to be So Damn Clever!

My penultimate piece of advice is more a word about what *not* to do. You will frequently see what I am about to dismiss being shared on hypnosis forums, and even taught by experienced trainers. This is the unfortunate practice of attempting to en-trance an analytical client by the use of clever language patterns and mind-bending language.

This is often explained as a technique to confound the conscious mind and thereby get straight-through to the subconscious. I even read a book not too long ago which

---

making any statement as to whether or not this is actually what is happening in the induction. See *ibid* for further discussion.

claimed that advanced use of this technique causes the mind to "shut down." No. No, it doesn't.

Other approaches view the conscious/subconscious model of the mind far too literally and suggest that it is possible to tie-up the conscious mind so effectively that it is helpless in blocking the suggestions that are fired at the subconscious. Even if such an approach was even vaguely accurate, it is hardly a collaborative or therapeutic way to work with fellow human beings![29]

I am risking overlap with the chapters on confusion, but I think that this applies just as much here. At least, it is an approach to confusion that is often employed against analyticals.[30] Unfortunately, these kind of techniques are often used by fresh enthusiastic students of hypnosis who have spent their hard-earned cash on the latest DVD, or training course, that promises them the secret weapons to hypnotise anyone at any time. They then become emotionally invested in the techniques that 1000 youtube videos convince them are effective and they pass on the ideas to others without giving it a second thought.

The sort of language you might encounter could include monstrosities such as, "You don't need to think about whatever it is that you are not thinking about right now... Sleep!" Or, even: "And I wonder how quickly you can pay no attention to that thing you are paying attention to now as you soon find that you are not focused on thinking about something now before you

---

29 In reality, this is little more than a revamping of techniques used in advertising to deliver subliminal messages to consumers. They have consistently been demonstrated to be ineffective.
30 And 'against' is sadly the correct word to use in this case.

haven't thought about something that you did not think about first then..."

Not only does this completely misunderstand the effective use of confusion, it fails at the first hurdle because rather than defeating the conscious mind it will be immediately flagged-up as patronising nonsense. Let us remember that subjects who habitually find themselves being analytical tend to be quite good at analysing things! When you add to that the unfamiliar experience of being hypnotised, you can almost guarantee that their minds are going to be hyper-vigilant, on the look out for anything that seems threatening, suspicious, appears out of place, or just does not make sense in some way.

Attempts to out-smart or bamboozle analytical clients and those like them are almost certainly doomed to failure. They are a sure-fire way to insult your client, have them put their guard up and immediately lose any rapport you had established. My suggestion is to stop trying to be clever and simply listen to your client. Pay attention to how their mind works and go with it. It may not be as impressive, but it's a damn sight more respectful.

Be Phenomenal!

This should be obvious by now, but it bears repeating as we close the chapter. Any time you are working with someone whose mind leans towards analysis, <u>use phenomena</u>. This applies to the pre-talk, the induction, the therapy and even after you bring them out of hypnosis.

It is important for analytical thinkers to believe that

they were hypnotised. As they are frequently in trance, they may not experience it in the same way that others do. Further, they may not be aware of it when it is experienced. If anything, they will feel exactly the same whether they are in hypnosis or out of it. So, these may be the clients who tend to say things like, "I did not feel as if I was in hypnosis." Therefore, the thing that will be a deciding factor for them is not how dissociated they felt, but anything else they experience that is interpreted as being hypnotic. Doubting that they have been in hypnosis is less of an issue when you have just taken them on a participatory experiential journey that involved their hand floating into the air and their foot being stuck to the floor!

If you take nothing else from the advice in this chapter, take this: Phenomena is key with analytical thinkers.

EXERCISE

What is your experience with so-called analyticals?

What would you say is the thing that makes analytical clients more difficult to hypnotise?

How might you utilise this, rather than confront it?

GRAHAM OLD

HYPNOSIS WITH THE HARD TO HYPNOTISE

Transcript of Sensory Overlap

Sensory Overload Inductions are a classic way to work with so-called analytical clients. Usually, the hypnotist uses whatever is happening around them, directing the client to focus on each input as it occurs, without giving them time to deal with any one sensation before moving on. The theory is that the analytical mind is overwhelmed with trying to keep up with everything, gives up and retreats into trance.

There are a few problems with this approach. Firstly, it does not take account of people's descriptions of what it is like to be overloaded. Secondly, it relies on the assumption that the hypnotist will be able to out-run the client. And finally, it requires the hypnotist to function in a way that may not be the most therapeutic.

The example transcript that follows is slightly different to the usual presentation of this induction. In this case, the analytical client's ability to "over-think" is utilised. Rather than seeking to overcome the client's brain, this version of a sensory overload embraces it. We have called this variation *Sensory Overlap*.

Common examples of this type of induction might be seen as seeking a break-down moment, a sort of crash when the overload has become unbearable and the client seeks refuge in trance. That is not the case here. In this version, the overlap is used as a means of leading the client gently back down to a state of calm.

You might think of the overlap in this induction as like the muscle tension that takes place in some versions of a Progressive Muscle Relaxation. The tension in itself is not the goal. Neither is it meant to be so painful that the client avoids it. Instead, the tension offers a comparison and in fact a spring-board to the relaxation.

In this induction, the overlap is like the application of tension. Then, as more items are added, the tension increases a little, then a little more, then there is a brief mention of relaxation as more tension is applied, then the tension increases, then a little more... and then a long slow sigh is let out as the tension gradually subsides, as more and more items are let go, until the only focus that remains is on the resulting relaxation, which the client sinks deeply into.

There is no uncomfortable breakdown, or retreating into trance, just a gradual increase of sensory input that provides a pleasant experience as it is all reversed.

> Hypnotist: "Take as much time as you need to get comfortable in that chair... I am going to be talking about various things and you might want to keep track of them... or you might not... it's up to you..."
>
> [The hypnotist is talking mainly on the client's exhalations, almost from the beginning.]
>
> H: "I don't know if you will be able to

concentrate on what I am saying better with your eyes open, or closed... so you can go ahead and do whatever is most comfortable to you..."

[Client closes eyes.]

H: "And as you relax into that comfort, I am going to invite you to pay attention to the sound of my voice... and to notice the sound of the words that I am using... As I'm talking to you, you might even picture the words that I am saying... perhaps you can imagine me writing them down as you think about the shape of the words... and hear my pen or pencil scratching on the paper as I make the shape of those words with my writing...

"As we go on, you can become aware of the other sounds around you... the gentle in and out of your own breath... the sounds close-by... the ticking of that clock in the background... the creaks and groans of the heating system... as well as the sounds outside that come and go... those every-day normal sounds that tell us that life goes on as usual... as you continue to listen to the sound of my voice and the sounds of my words...

"And as you allow yourself to rest in that chair... settling into that comfort... you may also become aware of how you are sitting... your feet flat on the floor... your hands resting on your lap... as you pay attention to the sounds of my voice and notice the sound of the words that I am using... As you imagine me writing these words down and the sound of the shape of these words... you can be aware of the sounds close-by... and the sounds outside that come and go... as you listen to the sound of my voice...

"And I don't know how aware you are of your body in the chair... as you feel the back of the chair on your back and the weight of your legs and how your arms are lying relaxed in your lap... as your body relaxes, your arms and legs getting heavy... as you hear the sound of my voice...

"And you might even become aware of the feeling of your feet on the floor... and they may feel numb and heavy... or how they usually feel, as you relax... aware of the sounds and words around you, relaxing your arms and your legs...

"You might focus on your breathing now... aware of how your breath is allowing you to naturally and effortlessly... relax more and more.. to let go and go deeper and deeper as you relax into the chair now... your shoulders loosening, your muscles relaxing, as your feet and arms and legs relax... and the sound of the world outside continues... with the sounds of the heating and the ticking of the clock... and the sound of my voice and the shape of my words... whilst you relax now deeper and deeper...

[The hypnotist's voice is now slowing down, reflecting the gradual reversal of the earlier energised overloaded state.]

"And maybe those gentle steady breaths can remind you of those times you ignore everything... as you settle down to sleep, to let go... and allow your mind to drift away... dreaming, sinking, floating... like a dream-cloud taking over, enjoying the feeling of release... and calm...

"Everything can settle down in its own time... settling comfortably now, those sounds relaxing you... soothing you... as you pay attention to the sound of my voice and your body continues to relax... deeper and deeper... sinking further and further, into that pleasant dream...

"nothing to do now... except drifting down and enjoying the feeling... how easily you let go when you want to go...

"more and more relaxed... feeling your whole body... as you focus on your breathing... sinking deeper and deeper into that relaxation...

"And that relaxation can drop into your feet... nice and heavy and relaxed... and you can notice that your thighs and your knees and your calves and your feet and your toes feel heavy... nice and heavy and relaxed... And you can sink into that and enjoy it...

"And if you would like to... you could even imagine those feet being too heavy to lift... as you allow yourself to enjoy that relaxation... and go ahead and imagine that... knowing what it would feel like... if your legs were too relaxed to lift... if your feet were so heavy they could not be lifted... sinking further into the ground... enjoy that feeling and embrace it... and if you want to feel that feeling even further, when you... know that your feet are too relaxed, too heavy to lift... you can go ahead and try and lift those feet... as you do, finding that it helps you sink into that relaxation... finding that they just feel heavier and heavier..."

[Client smiles as they appear to attempt to lift their feet.]

"And then you can just stop trying... and let

go... and let that pleasant calm relaxation... spread throughout your body and mind... that's it..."

EXERCISE

How do you feel about sensory overload inductions?

Is the Sensory Overlap a valid variation on the theme, or a completely different approach?

Is there a genuine difference between the two, or is it merely a difference in attitude?

Practice both the Sensory Overload and Sensory Overlap inductions. Get feedback from your practice-partners on how they found the experience.

Does the feedback you received influence which version you are most likely to use?

Confusion

Milton Erickson is well known for his use of confusion. The thing that may not be as well known is his insistence that all good hypnotic techniques involve an *element* of confusion.[31]

If you have only encountered confusion as part of an explicit 'confusion induction' then Erickson's statement may seem to be a wild exaggeration. However, there is more to confusion than a specific induction. In language that may be both confusing and hypnotic, Erickson wrote:

> Defined simply, a "confusion technique" is one based upon the presentation to the subjects of a series of seemingly only loosely related ideas actually based upon a significant thread of continuity not readily recognized, leading to an increasing divergence of associations, interspersed with an emphasis on the obvious, all of which preclude subjects from developing any one train of associations, yet stirs them increasingly to a need to do something until they are ready to accept the first clear-cut

---

31 Erickson writes, in *Hypnotic Realities*, 'In all my techniques, almost all, there is confusion,' p. 85. He later expands on that to state, '[Confusion] is the basis of all good techniques,' p. 107.

definitive suggestion offered. As stated, the technique may be purely verbal or an admixture of verbal and nonverbal elements; both may be used as rapid or slow inductions, depending upon the situation and the purposes to be served.[32]

A popular conception of *the* confusion induction is a series of apparently meaningless statements that tie-up someone's mind in a logical quest for relief, which they find by slipping in to trance. However, we can see here that not only can confusion be used in a non-verbal manner, but that it is actually made up of *meaningful* statements that simply open up too many avenues to keep track of.

Erickson's idea is to present 'a series of seemingly only loosely related ideas actually based upon a significant thread of continuity not readily recognized, leading to an increasing divergence of associations.' It that sense, the client is almost encouraged to keep up, as he can tell that sensible points are being made. However, just as he is beginning to decipher one point, another related point is made. Moreover, each of these points *require something* from the client, meaning that automatic translation is not always possible.

As an example of the latter, the hypnotist does not just say, for example, "hypnosis is like a pleasant daydream..." Instead, he is more likely to state something like, "you may find that hypnosis is like one of your

---

[32] Erickson, "The Dynamics of Visualization, Levitation and Confusion in Trance Induction," p. 2. in *The Collected Papers of Milton H. Erickson on Hypnosis, Vol. 1: Nature of Hypnosis and Suggestion.*

daydreams, perhaps like a dream you had at school one day, when your mind drifts from time to time during a lesson..." Statements like the latter require the client to go on an internal search to make sense of what is being said.

However, it can be far more straightforward than this. To simply say, "You know what it feels like to relax..." has more of an internal direction than, "When people relax..." The former is preferable because the client will go 'inside' to be able to accurately make sense of what is being said. They will then only just have translated the statement when a new one is being offered.

This understanding of confusion requires that the hypnotist present as sensible and logical at all other times. This is an essential point, yet sadly often neglected. If the client is accustomed to you going off on flights of fancy that lead to nowhere, they will not be inclined to follow you. However, if they are used to you making sense then they will follow where you lead, seeking-out the sensible resolution to what you are saying. They follow you precisely because they know you must be making sense (even if they are temporarily bewildered), because you always do.

Understood in this way, Erickson explains the goal of confusion as 'the pressing need to have a definite, easily comprehended understanding of what is wanted.' As such, 'the subject is more than ready to accept and react to the first simple idea suggested that will end the confusion.'[33]

In short, confusion creates attention and receptivity as your client listens for the next statement that makes

---

33 Ibid, p. 3.

sense. Thus, you achieve a state of anticipatory focus. It is easy, therefore, to see why Erickson considered it to be such a valuable tool.

In a later chapter, I will question much of the way that confusion is commonly used in hypnosis today. However, for now it is useful to toe the party line and present the popular position on this topic. My hope is that readers will make up their own minds and be equipped to act on this, regardless of which position they eventually adopt.

What is Confusion?

If we work backwards, we can come to a clear understanding of what confusion in a hypnotic context entails. It is:

> Any statement or action which creates attention and receptivity as your client waits for the next statement (or action) that makes sense, thereby achieving a state of anticipatory focus.

We will turn shortly to consider the various types of confusion. However, this definition is enough to demonstrate that confusion can be verbal or non-verbal. As Rubin Battino writes, the 'confusion induction can be a play on words and/or unexpected behaviour that interrupts usual thought patterns.'[34]

It should be obvious by now that we are not merely speaking of the confusion induction. Instead, we are

---
34 Battino, *Ericksonian Approaches*, p. 237.

looking at the use of confusion within an induction. It is often more useful to pepper an induction with confusion at different points than to attempt to compose a whole induction based on the confusion technique. It may be more effective to use confusion to lead the client towards meaningful statements. In that sense, the non-confusing statements almost function like embedded commands, as they jump out and demand the attention of the client's now receptive mind.

There are a number of ways that confusion may be used in a hypnotic induction:

Sensory confusion

Any lack of clarity regarding sensory input provides a moment of confusion. A common example of this is what some refer to as a double induction, with words being spoken into each ear at the same time. This category also includes occasions when someone may be hearing something whilst also seeing something and not being certain which input to focus on. Some people would consider techniques like EMDR or EFT to be examples of this.

Sensory Overload

An extension of the above is sensory overload. Someone's attention can be focused on evaluating sensory inputs to exclusion of all else. The client is encouraged to focus on each input as it occurs, without giving them time to deal with any one sensation before moving on to the next.

Non sequiturs

A non sequitur is a statement presented in the form of 'cause (A) leads to effect (B)', but where there is no logical connection between A and B. Sometimes, the connection may feel vaguely logical, whereas at other times it will be obvious that there is no real connection.

For example, "As you close your eyes, you will find that you can more easily notice that relaxation increasing," or, "You can hear the relaxing sound of my voice, causing that arm to feel lighter and lighter."

Homonyms

Arm levitation inductions often rely on homonyms such as: "And I don't know if your right arm will begin to raise, meaning that the other arm is left. Or if your other arm will be right for you and your right arm will be left..."

Double entendres

Use of double entendres is another example of linguistic confusion. It can lead to a brief moment of uncertainty in the hearer's mind, as they work to discern which particular meaning of the word is being used.

Oppositional Pairs

Using oppositional pairs may involve word groups such as now/then, here/there and conscious/unconscious.

"So you can sit there... in that chair here... while you try, to be aware of the exact meaning... of the words you hear... and of all the changes... that occur there... in your thoughts, sensations or awareness... as I speak here."[35]

---

[35] Ronald Havens, *Hypnotherapy Scripts: A Neo-Ericksonian Approach to Persuasive Healing*, p. 65.

Associational Confusion

Associational confusion takes place when it is not clear what the target of a sentence is. This may occur in the case of double entendres, or run-on sentences. A common usage involves the word "now." For example:

> *And as you begin to think about the changes you are making at a subconscious level... now... you can take a deep breath...*

This may also take place if e.g. the hypnotist is telling a story and it is not clear who is being referred to, or in some nested loops, or some variations of My Friend John.

Shifting States

Associating someone into a state, then dissociating them, then associating again, with unclear boundaries between the two can lead to a strong experience of confusion. Shifting states can be thought of as the emotional equivalent of sensory overload.

Kinaesthetic Confusion

Confusion involving the body can take many forms. Even something as simple as Magnetic Hands can create a light confusion, as people are baffled or amused by what is happening to them. Alternatively, an arm levitation may evoke the same response. A slight rocking motion is considered by some to create a regressive experience, where the client relives early parental nurture. However, it is also possible that the rhythmic movements create a sense of bodily uncertainty, a confusion as to what is taking place, no matter how comforting it may be.

A postural sway, arm drop or muscle catalepsy create a sense of uncertainty as to what is being experienced. It is as if the rules of normal bodily experience are up in the air and the hypnotee searches for clarification or new direction.

Pattern-interrupt

A pattern-interrupt occurs any time we break a conditioned process before the expected conclusion is reached. This can be sensory, verbal, or physical. It almost always induces a moment of confusion and anticipatory focus.

Why Use Confusion and With Whom?

The outcome of confusion discussed above – 'attention and receptivity... a state of anticipatory focus' – is enough to justify the use of confusion in the induction of hypnosis. However, there are any number of means to achieve such ends. Why is confusion in particular worth mastering?

In the magnificent *Hypnotic Realities*, Ernest Rossi and Erickson discuss the use of confusion:

> R: You said earlier that in almost all your induction techniques, confusion is something that breaks up their reality orientation. It breaks their tie to normal awakeness?[36]

---

36 Erickson, *Hypnotic Realities*, p. 89.

Erickson agrees, noting that confusion leads to an uncertainty about yourself and your situation. Rossi questions if confusion could not then be seen as 'an opening wedge to trance.'

> E: Yes. If you are uncertain about yourself, you can't be certain about anything else.
>
> R: Actually they are getting a lot of their reality sense from you and if you throw doubt into them?
>
> E: It spills over into their doubt about all reality.[37]

We begin to see here the importance of confusion. It is so powerful, when employed skilfully, that it can cause someone to 'doubt about all reality.' The discussion continues:

> R: So can we make a summary statement that the basis of good hypnotic induction is confusion?
>
> E: Confusion about the surrounding reality which in ordinary life is always clear. If the surrounding reality becomes unclear, they want it cleared up by being told something (e.g., I

---
37 Ibid.

don't know where I am in this city: where am I? I don't recognize this place: what is it?).³⁸

We are now getting to the heart of the use of confusion. When someone begins to doubt their own reality – experiencing what Erickson describes as, the 'dimming of outer reality' – they start looking for some clarity. People look for clarification, or direction, to make sense of their current experience.

This is often described as someone trying to 'escape' from their confusion. There are hints of this in the discussion between Rossi and Erickson:

> E: If you are uncertain about something, you tend to avoid it.
>
> R: I see! They start withdrawing from reality if they are uncertain about it.
>
> E: That's right! They don't know what it [reality] is.
>
> R: If you then add to that the suggestion of a pleasant inner reality, they'd rather go to it.
>
> E: Anything is better than that state of doubt.³⁹

The idea seems to be that because 'anything is better

---
38 Ibid., p. 90.
39 Ibid. P. 89.

than the state of doubt,' if you give someone the suggestion to go elsewhere – e.g. into trance – they will take it to escape the confusion. Whether or not such a description would match what people actually experience, I will leave for others to argue. However, the general idea has merit. If we are confused, it seems to be the case that we naturally and consistently seek to rectify the confusion. As such, we are more likely to accept any statement or action that appears to provide relief from the confusion.

In a section entitled, *Depotentiating Conscious Mental Sets: Confusion, Mental Flux, And Creativity*, Rossi sheds some light on the type of situation where confusion might be used:.

> Confusion...is used to detach people from their "conscious mental sets." You have broken the connections that might have been stopping them from working on their problem. A patient is a patient because of erroneous mental sets and limited frames of reference. Erickson continually seeks to break through these rigid limitations to initiate a state of mental flux that may release the patient's creative potential.[40]

Seen in this way, confusion can be employed to function as a powerful mechanism for breaking rigid mental sets and initiating psychological flexibility.

For some people, their mental sets are too fixed to provide the necessary movement needed to think creatively, let alone engage with any of the resources that

---
40 Ibid., p.151.

may be discovered through trance. We might say that they have an overly static understanding of reality and their relationship to it. Confusion might then be employed to 'dim' their current reality through a momentary uncertainty as to the way things are. This provides hypnotists a brief window to introduce fresh ideas and new directions, as well as allowing clients the experience of a more flexible mental set.

We will explore this further in later chapters.

EXERCISE

Ernest Rossi wrote:

'A patient is a patient because of erroneous mental sets and limited frames of reference.'

Do you agree?

If so, what are the implications for how you work with people?

Do you think the idea of 'erroneous mental sets and limited frames of reference' can be said to apply to hypnotists and hypnotherapists?

GRAHAM OLD

HYPNOSIS WITH THE HARD TO HYPNOTISE

Typical Confusion Induction Transcript

The following transcript is offered as an example of a fairly typical Confusion Induction.[41]

> Sometimes we can find ourselves paying attention... to the most relaxing things. So you can sit there... in that chair here... listening with your subconscious mind, while your conscious mind remains very relaxed and peaceful. You can relax peacefully... while you try to be aware... of the exact meaning of the words you hear... and of all the changes that occur there... in your thoughts, sensations or awareness... as I speak here.
>
> Or you can forget about trying... to make all the unnecessary effort... to pay close attention... to everything that happens. Because you can remember that you can forget so easily... and with forgetting certain things you can remember other things... Remembering what you need to remember... and forgetting what you can forget... It does

---

[41] This transcript is taken from my website, howtodoinductions.com. It incorporates a number of elements found in various induction scripts.

not matter if you forget... you need not remember. Your subconscious mind remembers everything that you need to know... and you can let your subconscious mind listen... and remember while... your conscious mind sleeps and forgets... And all you really need to do... is remember that your memory is for getting... things that you thought you had forgotten.

So you can forget about trying... to make the effort... to pay close attention... to everything that happens... or does not happen... in your experience... as you listen to me... and also to your own thoughts... or to your sensations... that change over time... or stay the same... in an arm or an ear... and your legs or fingers.

And what about the thoughts... and the variety of images... that speak to your mind's eye... as I speak to your mind... to remind you that what you speak to yourself... speaks for itself... as you try to search and find that things... may seem to be one thing... but turn out to be another.

Because two and two are four, but two can also... mean also... and no two are alike. It all belongs to you...

and to your own ability... to relax... those two ears too... and to begin to know that you really don't know... what means yes... and what means no, here... though you may try to guess... where you're going... to go or not to go... you don't know... that there is no... real way to know... how to let go while holding on... or to recognise... that there is nothing you need to try to know... to do or not to do... because everything you do... allows you to recognise that you already know that... I can say many different things... and there is no need for you to make the effort it takes... to try to make the effort to pay close attention... to each thing I say or don't say, because there was a time when the effort to train the mind to stay on track... was not worth the trip that led the mind back to that time... of peaceful... calm awareness... of effortless letting go... getting low and knowing that you don't need to try to hear or even understand... what I might say later on here today... because the conscious mind... can go anywhere it wishes while I continue to talk... and your unconscious mind continues to hear... that way you overhear... a conversation... or a radio station... while driving.

You don't even need to do anything at all. It all belongs to you as you begin to hear... the way you do... here and now... with eyes closed... comfortable... that voice or sound... in the background... of the mind... as you listened to that show... show that too... and it showed you how to notice the relaxed... drifting glow... of a slow... sound show... of quiet calmness... and thoughts like dreams... following themselves... as I spoke

turning... spokes in wheel turning... this way and that, where we'll be drifting... effortlessly down a path... into a quiet still place where words... can remind... your mind... of those things needed for you.

Other times we drift a bit... as we think about all the things that are parallel in the universe... and all the things... which cross across the horizons of those parallel things... but we always find ourselves slowing down for a stop sign... and drifting... floating... below the threshold of our consciousness.

When we feel ourselves let go of those parallel line thoughts... and just focus on how drifting... seems effortless... in a timeless drifting down motion... which we find many times to be relaxing... relaxing, relaxing deeper... and deeper... as we add three plus three plus three plus... the horizon of relaxation... in a drifting feeling as we float along to the solution... which relaxes us deeper into the concepts that we are now examining... because four plus four is forethought to forgo consciousness... and drifting happens when we now calculate all of the foregoing thoughts... in the parallel sphere of our own reality... letting go... and relaxing deeper and deeper.

Hasn't it always been that way?... As you look at things in a different light, of course... you can see now that there is always a different way... And there always has been... it's just that sometimes it's the same way that you already know... And as you weigh that up... it can be quite relaxing for your mind to... find that way down.

On the other hand... one plus one is two of a kind... and a straight flush down the river, rowing a boat on a relaxing day... and getting very tired of rowing and rows and rows of hay in a field having been bailed by a male that sails down the same river... and lets go of the drifting current currently... relaxing in the warm sunshine... relaxing in a chair there... like walking down stairs... deeper and deeper.

EXERCISE

Do you / would you use a confusion induction?

Write your own version of a confusion induction and practice it with someone.

Get feedback from them on how they found the experience.

Consider how *you* found the experience.

Are there things you would do differently, or re-write, based on the feedback you received?

How to Use Confusion

Gilligan's Precept

When it comes to *how* we can employ confusion, few people have expressed this as well as Stephen Gilligan. As a result, I have come to refer to the following description – a basic statement as to the appropriate use of confusion – as Gilligan's Precept:

> Confusion techniques utilise whatever the client is doing to inhibit trance or other therapeutic developments *as the basis for inducing those developments*.[42]

This could not be more important and is a principle that the following chapter will show is central to my use of confusion. Contrary to how confusion is often presented, perhaps as a means to bypass or defeat someone's mind, confusion works *with* their mind. However, we may be getting ahead of ourselves.

For now, let's limit ourselves to a description of *how* we use confusion. Applying Gilligan's Precept to the induction of hypnosis, it suggests that the effective use of confusion uses the actual thing that a client may be doing to inhibit

---
42 S. Gilligan, *Therapeutic Trances*, p.236. Emphasis mine.

hypnosis as the very basis for inducing hypnosis. So, how do we make sense of this?

We could return to Erickson's description of limiting 'mental sets' and recognise that someone's inflexible thinking may be hindering their experience of hypnosis. Therefore, rather than ignoring this information, we use it to our (and their!) advantage. This could involve helping clients explore the limitations of their mental processes, perhaps facilitating a sense of frustration at their own inflexibility. Or, it could involve intentionally introducing them to ideas or experiences that we know will not fit with their current mental set, to see if they are tempted to knock down the walls to explore them further.

Someone else may be continually over-thinking, with a racing mind. We can then choose to ignore this, resist it, or work with it. We might encourage them to use this thinking pattern and race to their heart's content, fairly certain that at some point they are going to have to stop to catch their breath.

Similarly, when we were discussing so-called analytical subjects, we saw how their tendency to "over-analyse" can be a skill that is utilised for their own good. Not only do we allow them to analyse, we encourage them to analyse all the way in to another trance!

So, we are taking the thinking process or pattern of behaviour that appears to be a conflict with our induction and we allow it to transform how we are seeking to induce hypnosis. To quote Gilligan once again:

> The most effective confusion techniques are those that use the very pattern that is keeping the person out of trance as the basis for the

induction. Again, whatever the person is doing is exactly that which will allow him to experience trance.[43]

The Confusion Framework

There are a number of ways to outline the practical implementation of confusion. The following is a composite of the frameworks provided by Erickson and Gilligan. I have found it to be an effective way to approach the use of this powerful mechanism. This is by no means the only way to use confusion in an induction, but it does seem to provide a fairly accurate summary of how confusion is often used when it is employed effectively.

1. Identify the Process

We begin by identifying a dominant behaviour pattern or thought-process in the client's life.

2. Initiate the Process

Returning to the analogy of Aikido, this would be *blending* with the process. Those familiar with NLP might see it as pacing the current behaviour.

3. Confuse the Process

This generally occurs through interrupting or overloading the process in such a way that it confuses the client.

---
43 S. Gilligan. *The Legacy of Milton H. Erickson: Selected Papers of Stephen Gilligan*, p.13

4. Extend the Confusion

This language is once again employing the aikido analogy. In this case, we are briefly prolonging – and thereby almost certainly amplifying – the confusion.

5. Utilise the Confusion

This is where the hypnotist uses the confusion, perhaps by introducing a simple suggestion (for example, "let go"), or offering an alternative experience (such as trance, or relaxation). Within the aikido comparison, this is the stage where the opponent's movement and energy has been blended, extended to the point that they are losing balance – and this is simply letting them fall.

Taking these five steps, we can examine some examples of confusion and see the framework in action. Let's start with a simple Bandler Handshake,[44] which is a 'pattern interrupt' variation of confusion. Adhering to Gilligan's Precept, this may have been chosen because it was observed that the client is preoccupied with social norms and an adherence to custom. Or, they may have shown themselves to be someone with an overly rigid model of the world, or their role within it.

1. A simple handshake is identified as something of an automatic social process.

2. The hypnotist offers his hand to initiate the handshake.

---

[44] See http://www.howtodoinductions.com/inductions/bandler for an example.

HYPNOSIS WITH THE HARD TO HYPNOTISE

The client naturally responds – usually with very little conscious thought – by reaching out their own hand to begin the handshake.

3. Just as the two hands are about to touch, the hypnotist may withdraw his own hand slightly, interrupting the handshake. Before the client has time to contemplate what is taking place – and certainly before they have considered removing their hand – the hypnotist uses his other hand to take the client's hand by the wrist and he lifts the hand up in front of his face.

4. The client is instructed to focus on their hand, which may cause blurring of the eyes as it moves closer to their face.

5. Depending on how the induction proceeds, the confusion may be utilised to create a catalepsy in the arm, or simply offering the invitation to go in to hypnosis as the arms floats or drops down.

As you can see, the Bandler Handshake provides a good demonstration of the applicability of the 5-step framework. Another example may further support the idea.

1. A client may be observed to fidget excessively, or be overly focused on their kinaesthetic sensations.

2. The client is invited to try the other chair and see if they find it more comfortable.

3. Not long after the client has sat down, they are asked to return to the first chair and compare it. Then, just as they are sitting down, they are instructed back to the second chair.

4. The rate of switching between chairs is increased, until the client becomes quiet tired or disoriented.

5. Finally, the client is invited to sit down and close their eyes, allowing themselves to sink into trance as they sink into the chair.

One more example will hopefully cement the idea. This involves an overload induction.

1. It may be decided that a particular client is easily distracted by their environment, as much as by their own self-reported "over-thinking."

2. The client is directed to notice their environment, whilst also being instructed to think about a number of things.

3. The number of items that the client is told to notice increases, along with the internal observations they are invited to make. It begins to become impossible for them to keep-up with all of the things in their surroundings and internal experience that they are asked to notice.

4. The overloading of internal and external attention and awareness is continued beyond the point at which it became unsustainable.

5. Eventually, the overloaded client is encouraged to hone in on one simple thought, such as relaxation.

These three examples demonstrate that the 5-step framework appears to work well as a description of how to effectively use confusion.

Know your Audience

Hopefully, the examples used above have also served to reiterate that this is all about utilisation. This is not simply a case of using a confusion induction because it is a favourite of yours, or because you fancied a change. It is equally not something that I think can be prepared ahead of time before you have met your client, or got to know them.

Respectful use of confusion requires rapport and trust on the part of your client. Fail to establish that and you are likely to do little more than generate frustration, annoyance and even distress. If there is any suspicion in our client's minds that we respect them and believe them to be unique, intelligent and resourceful, we run the risk that our employment of confusion will be seen as a means of ridiculing or otherwise intellectually besting someone.

In this regard, it is useful to remind ourselves of the purpose of using confusion during an induction. Confusion is used to assist the client to disengage with the rigid limits of their usual way of being and thinking. It enables the people we are privileged to work with to discover more flexibility in their mental sets.

It is this respect for clients that causes my own

discomfort with much of the use of confusion that I encounter. This is the reason behind my own rethinking of the use of confusion, which I will turn to now as we draw this topic to a close.

EXERCISE

We have described the Confusion Framework as:

1. Identify the Process

2. Initiate the Process

3. Confuse the Process

4. Extend the Confusion

5. Utilise the Confusion

Do you find this to be a helpful description of the use of confusion?

Re-write the framework, using your own words.

GRAHAM OLD

Rethinking Confusion

I was originally taught that the only really reliable way to work with analytical or resistant clients was to confuse them. This took the form of speaking in endless sentences, employing all kinds of clever language patterns, with the intention of wrapping their mind up in trying to make sense of whatever I said. The idea was that my client would get so confused that they would jump to accept the first meaningful thing that was said to them. If that meaningful thing was a suggestion to go into trance, into trance they would go!

I have to say that such an approach *can* work. However, after following this advice for many years, I have now come to the conclusion that it is in fact a lousy way to treat people. It is actually somewhat surprising that it took me so long to come to this conclusion. As it happens, confusion inductions have never worked on me and I would be considered an 'analytical' client. I've always found them frustrating and it would seem that I am not the only one.

Questioning Confusion

In 2012, a study by the University of Notre Dame concluded that contrary to what we might presume, confusion *can* actually be beneficial to learning something, if – and this is the important bit – *if* the confusion is *ultimately resolved*.[45] Yet, what we often see with confusion inductions is the confusion being escaped from, *not* resolved. In fact, this escape is often touted as the very reason to use confusion inductions in the first place.

Rather than being an experience to learn from, confusion becomes an annoyance to be avoided. This is not a new discovery. Erickson records the reaction of one client:

> "I have always felt somewhat annoyed and distressed by the Confusion Technique, and I have resented its use, but initially I was willing to listen and cooperate as best I could. Part of my resentment was undoubtedly due to my own mental pattern of thought; I always like to grasp each idea and organize my thoughts before proceeding. However, I went along with the confusion suggestions and I know they worked on me, although not as well as other techniques did.
>
> "At the present time they will not work on me. No matter how deep a trance I am in and how cooperative I am, I simply stop listening if that type of suggestion is begun. Nor will I make any pretence of listening. If the operator insists on keeping on talking, I shut off my hearing

---

45 D'Mello, S., *Lehman*, B., Pekrun, R. & Graesser, A. (2014). *Confusion can be beneficial for learning. Learning* and Instruction, 29, 153-170.

(self-established hypnotic deafness) and I may wake up feeling strongly annoyed."[46]

Research conducted by Stanger, Tucker & Morgan found that confusion techniques were no more effective than a standard induction for low-susceptible subjects. Whilst it is unclear whether the low-susceptible subjects were analytical thinkers, it seems plausible to assume that at least some in that group would have been.[47]

In 1985, Kirsch, Matthews and Mosher examined the 'double induction' spoken of previously. The procedure usually involves two hypnotists speaking into a subject's ears (one speaking to the left, one speaking to the right). This had been promoted by Bandler and Grinder as superior to traditional hypnotic inductions.[48] Further, Lankton and Lankton[49] claimed that using such two-level communication and interspersing suggestions in a confusing dual induction produces superior results. Yet, the researchers found no significant differences between the double induction and a traditional one in terms of depth of trance or response to suggestion. In fact, it seems that the double induction may actually *decrease*

---

46 Erickson, *The Confusion Technique in Hypnosis*. The American Journal of Clinical Hypnosis, January, 1964, 6, 183-207.
47 Thomas Stanger, Carolyn M. Tucker & James I. Morgan. *The Impact of a Confusion Technique on Hypnotic Responsivity in Low-Susceptible Subjects*. American Journal of Clinical Hypnosis, Volume 38, 1996 - Issue 3.
48 They described it as "one of the most powerful induction and deepening techniques." Bandler, R., & Grinder, J. (1975). *Patterns of the hypnotic techniques of Milton H. Erickson, M.D. (Vol. 1)*. Cupertino, CA: Meta Publications, p. 196
49 Lankton, S., & Lankton, C. (1983). *The answer within: A clinical framework of Ericksonian hypnotherapy*. New York: Brunner Mazel Publishers, Inc.

hypnotic responsiveness in some subjects![50]

How then do we account for the anecdotal evidence suggesting that confusion inductions work well where all else fails, particularly for those with a more analytical thinking-style? There are a number of things to consider here. Firstly, it pains me to say so, but any anecdote that involves Erickson needs to be taken with a pinch of salt. This is not because they are necessarily inaccurate, but simply because he was Milton Erickson. After Erickson had reached a certain level of fame – often for using innovative hypnotic techniques – he was sought out by many for precisely that reason. Thus, it seems fair to assume that the great doctor could have said anything to many such visitors and they would have slipped into trance. When Erickson uttered confusing words it would have been a very clear signal that this was a hypnotic technique in action, prompting the expected response.

Secondly, some therapists turn to confusion techniques after having tried a number of other inductions unsuccessfully. It is certainly possible that by the time a confusion induction is employed, the client will have gone into and out of light trances enough times that any induction could have been used and effectively benefited from the previous fractionation.

Thirdly, confusion techniques certainly *do* work for some people. For example, Erickson records the experiences of two subjects:

> Miss H and Mr. T were excellent subjects for either traditional or the Confusion Techniques. However, after a few experiences with the

---

50 Matthews WJ, Kirsch I, Mosher D. *Double hypnotic induction: an initial empirical test*. Journal of Abnormal Psychology. 1985 Feb;94(1):92-5.

> Confusion Technique they reacted by bypassing it and developing a trance at once, no matter how subtly the author made his approach. As they would explain in the trance state, "As soon as I experienced the slightest feeling of confusion, I just dropped into a deep trance." They simply did not like to be confused. Neither of these subjects, fully capable with more common techniques, could seem to learn to use a Confusion Technique or even to outline a possible form. *There were others who responded similarly.*[51]

Practitioners of the confusion induction might celebrate this as an example of the induction working well. After all, the clients bypassed the confusion and 'dropped into a deep trance.' They escaped. However, note that 'they simply did not like to be confused.' This was not a pleasant experience for them. With such an experience, the induction becomes simply a tool to pressurise someone into trance. They gain nothing else from it. I may be wrong, but I hardly think this is an approach we should be promoting.

In my opinion, using confusion to befuddle someone into trance is often an outdated and non-therapeutic approach to inductions. Personally, I have no desire to cause someone to doubt themselves; quite the opposite. And I have no need to outsmart or out-analyse anyone. So, if someone has a strong and active mind, I want to

---

[51] Erickson, *The Confusion Technique in Hypnosis,* p. 198. Emphasis added. We might question if it was the clients failing to learn – as Erickson suggested – or Erickson himself!

help them use that to their advantage.

Is there a place for Confusion?

I'm aware that my thoughts on confusion are in opposition to much of the writing on the subject. So, allow me to provide an example of the kind of client with whom I may still use some elements of confusion.

If someone comes to see me and they are an experienced meditator they may appear to be an ideal candidate for hypnosis. Without a doubt, they will be experienced at going in to trance and their interest in the process will produce an internal analytical loop that can be easily utilised. However, there can be a downside to such a client and that is their tendency to want to assist the hypnotist. If they want to analyse everything that it happening at the conscious and subconscious level, I have not got a problem with that and it makes my job substantially easier. Yet, if they are trying to fulfil my role, rather than allowing themselves to experience what is taking place, we could have difficulties. As such, I tend to say that I use confusion for people whose mind gets in their own way.

I strongly reject the outdated notion of using confusion to practically bully someone into submission. I find such a battle-of the-wits idea to be unnecessary and unhelpful. In fact, it is a sure way to *increase* resistance and merely demonstrates that the hypnotist and the client are not on the same page. Instead, I believe that confusion is best employed as a temporary means of assisting clients to steer passed an obstacle that they themselves desire to bypass.

So, I would encourage you to use confusion as part of your collaborative interaction with people, as an example of client-centred utilisation. That's almost the opposite to the battle-of the-wits!

This may be the place to note that another reason why the battle of wits is unhelpful is that there is no guarantee that the hypnotist is going to win. If you do happen to be working with someone whose mind tends towards analysis, what makes you think that you are going to be able to stay one step ahead of them and confuse them into submission? They may very well keep up with everything you're saying and just end up annoyed at the nonsense you are wasting their time spouting.

Kinaesthetic Confusion

Of course, we should note that there is a difference between utilising confusion as an occasional technique and using it as the whole induction. Additionally, there are all sorts of ways that confusion can be employed. As we noted in a previous chapter, linguistic confusion is but one example.

I've talked about my distaste for how confusion is commonly used to deal with so-called analyticals. However, I should mention that one of the main ways I *do* still use aspects of confusion is by employing kinaesthetic confusion. In doing so, I am intentionally choosing concrete memorable *experiences* versus confusing *language*. I don't know about you, but I know which I'd rather be on the receiving end of!

A good example of kinaesthetic confusion is seen in

something like the Thain wrist-lift.[52] The sudden catalepsy can create a moment of confused anticipation, focus and expectancy as your client receives the strong impression that the usual rules do not currently apply.

When such an approach to inductions is undertaken effectively, there is no longer any need to fear the so-called analytical client. And confusion as a battle-of-the-wits becomes a thing of the past.

Rather than opposing someone's analytical mind, we can use the induction to lead them through an experiential process where they learn just how powerful their mind is. We can therefore begin to look forward to working with such clients, recognising that they bring great strengths to the hypnotic encounter. Instead of battling and belittling such powerful minds, let's welcome them and learn with them.

---

52 http://www.howtodoinductions.com/inductions/wristlift

EXERCISE

To what extent do you agree or disagree with the arguments against the use of confusion?

Present your own arguments for and against confusion as an induction tool.

What type of people, if any, do you consider most suited to experience confusion during an induction?

GRAHAM OLD

Kinaesthetic Confusion Transcript

The core of this unique induction was originally developed by Graham Wicks. This is a rapid hypnotic technique, devoid of any shock. It is phenomenological at its core and relies upon kinaesthetic confusion.

The original induction had the hypnotist keep hold of the client's hand (and lower it themselves), regardless of the presence or absence of catalepsy (seen in version 2 below). The modification added later was to allow the arm to float down on its own, if catalepsy was initially achieved (version 1).

The Modified Wicks Induction (version 1)

Hypnotist: "Are you left or right-handed?"

Client: "Right-handed."

H: "And it's fine for me to touch you on the wrist, as I lift up your arm?"

C: "Yeah."

H: "Brill. Thank you. And you have full movement and good health in your wrist, your arm, your shoulder?"

C: "Yeah, fine."

H: "And, last question, are you happy to go into hypnosis quite quickly this afternoon?"

C: "Yes, I am."

H: "Excellent. So…"

[Hypnotist takes the client's arm and fully extends it all the way above their head.]

H: "Close your eyes. Take a deep breath. Hold it…"

["Hold it" is said precisely as the hypnotist lets go of the arm almost completely, with it just resting on their thumb. They sense that the arm is cataleptic and staying up on its own. After a couple of seconds, they continue:]

"Let the breath out. And let the rest of your body relax completely… In a moment, your arm will slowly begin to float down to your lap. As it comes down, you will feel yourself going more and more deeply into hypnosis. But I don't want you to go all of the way in, until that hand has come to rest."

[As the arm begins to float down, say:]

"That's right, coming down only as quickly as you go deeper into hypnosis. The deeper you go, the better you feel. And the better you feel, the deeper you go. All the way..."

[Just as the hand is coming to rest in their lap, or by their side, say:]

"And you can go all of the way inside now. Every beat of your heart, every word that I say and every sound that you hear, causing you to go deeper and deeper..."

The Modified Wicks Induction (version 2)

Begin as in version 1.

[Hypnotist takes the client's arm and fully extends it all of the way above their head.]

H: "Close your eyes. Take a deep breath. Hold it..."

[If the client's arm is heavy, instead of being cataleptic, after a couple of seconds, continue:]

"Let the breath out. And let your body relax completely... Your arm is now deeply relaxed and heavy and it will get heavier and heavier as I allow it to descend. And as your arm moves down, you can go deeper and deeper into that relaxation. But I don't want you to go all the way into hypnosis, until that hand has come to rest."

[As you move the arm down, taking between 10 and 20 seconds, you may include words like:]

"That's right, getting heavier and heavier, going deeper and deeper. And the deeper you go, the better you feel. And the better you feel, the deeper you go."

[Once you have brought their hand all of the way down, say:]

"And you can go all of the way inside now. Deeply relaxed. Loose and limp. [Said as you drop the hand for the final half inch.] And every beat of your heart, every word that I say and every sound that you hear, causing you to go deeper and deeper."

EXERCISE

What do you think of the concept of kinaesthetic confusion?

Is this a helpful way to frame what is taking place within the Modified Wicks induction?

Practice using the Modified Wicks induction.

Get feedback on the induction. Consider also your own experience as the hypnotist.

Continue to practice the induction, perhaps adjusting to incorporate anything learned from your feedback.

GRAHAM OLD

Phenomenal Inductions

One of the frustrations that hypnotists sometimes speak of when working with analytical clients is not knowing if they were in hypnosis. This might be echoed by such clients, who open their eyes at the end of a session, unsure if they were simply going through the motions and if anything out of the ordinary actually took place.

Not so long ago, I heard a Hypnosis Trainer tell his audience that he no longer used convincers. His argument was that it was not his desire to force anyone to think that they were hypnotised. However, from my perspective, this takes the notion of 'convincers' a little too literally and thereby misunderstands their purpose.

The goal is not to force your understanding of an experience on your clients, or demand that they frame things a particular way. However, on the whole, our clients have come to us for hypnosis. So, rather than attempting to convince them that something happened when it did not, the role of phenomena is to help clients understand what is taking place and adjust their expectations and responses accordingly.

A number of studies have found that when a client believes they are experiencing hypnosis, rather than simply relaxing, or being given suggestions in their everyday state, the likelihood of them responding to suggestions increases greatly.[53] At the very least, hypnotic phenomena therefore functions less as a simple convincer and more as frame, a means of understanding the whole experience of hypnosis.

Phenomena is essential for clients who routinely reside in their head. This is not necessarily so they can have logical proof that they were in hypnosis. If they were so inclined, I'm sure they could unpick any hypnotic phenomena and dispute that it provides irrefutable evidence that they were in hypnosis.

Phenomena is not strictly a 'convincer' in that sense. It is not going to persuade any sceptics, for instance. However, that is not what most clients are looking for. Few clients visit us with an attitude of, "prove it!" After all, they have sought us out and are paying for our services. In practically every case, they want to believe.

So, whilst phenomena may not necessarily equate to cast-iron evidence, that is not to downplay its value. Phenomena, to use Erickson's language, provides a 'dimming of outer reality.' It introduces a moment where the usual rules do not apply. Reality suddenly becomes pliable and as a result another world becomes possible.

Let's consider some inductions that have phenomena at their very core.

The Sinking Spot

The Sinking Spot induction is a variation of the classic eye-fixation. It includes a built-in hallucination and uses

---

53 Cf. Gandhi B, et al. *Does 'hypnosis' by any other name smell as sweet? The efficacy of 'hypnotic' inductions depends on the label 'hypnosis'.* Consciousness and Cognition, Volume 14, Issue 2, June 2005, Pp. 304-315.

the physical occurrence of eyes lowering to suggest going 'deeper' into a hypnotic experience.

> Hypnotist: "All you need to do is keep your head still and follow my finger-tips with your eyes. Okay?"
>
> Client: "Okay."
>
> H: "Right, so, look here..."
>
> [Hypnotist holds up his hand at eye-level in front of the client, his hand in a Cub Scout salute, with his forefinger and middle finger pointing straight-up. He taps the fingertips of his upright fingers, to emphasise where the client is to focus.]
>
> H: "I am going to move my fingers back and forth like this..."
>
> [Hypnotist waves his arm in front of the client, from left to right, causing the client to look fully to the left and fully to the right.]
>
> H: "And up and down, like this..."
>
> [Hypnotist moves his arm down, in line with the centre of his client's body, until the client's eyes are fully extended looking down.]

H: "And you can just keep your head comfortably resting and still, following along with your eyes only. Okay?"

C: "Yeah."

[The hypnotist then moves their hand all the way along the horizontal axis, from the far left to right, twice. Encouragements such as, "that's right," or "keep following," are offered from time to time.

After the horizontal axis has been covered twice, when the hypnotist next reaches the centre, he then moves his hand down and up again.]

H: "Now, up and down, that's it..."

[The hypnotist is effectively drawing a large upper-case T in the air. This is repeated twice more.

As the hypnotist's hand comes up for the third and final time, the hand comes up slightly higher than the client's eye-line and then taps the air firmly.]

H: "See that spot staying there, floating in the air. You might picture it as a coloured dot, or a small ball... [The hypnotist takes his fingers away, as he says...] keep your eyes resting on that spot.

H: "And as you focus on it, I don't know if it is solid or transparent. Perhaps it is a 3D sphere, like a marble, or flat like a coin or a sticker. However, you see it, rest your eyes on that spot.

[Hypnotist begins to match the client's breathing.]

"It may be that the colour changes, as your focus shifts in and out. Perhaps you notice more detail. It may be textured, I don't know. Or it may begin to blur and wobble slightly.

"And while you keep looking at that spot, wondering around it but coming back to it with your eyes in a gentle easy going comfortable way, you can become aware of the muscles around your eyes... how they they are holding your eyes up... that's right... and your eyelids... and what they feel like...

"You may [wait for them to blink] blink a bit more frequently [wait for them to blink again] that's right... and your breathing might get deeper, as you relax.

"And after some time, you might notice as the spot seems to be too heavy to stay up any longer. It may start sinking, slowly, slowly, ever so slowly down.

"And you can follow it with your eyes... as it moves slowly lower and lower, as it gets heavier and heavier.

"You may have already noticed that as that spot gets heavier, you can be aware of your body relaxing deeper and deeper, your eyes heavier, moving lower and lower.

"And blinking [wait for them to blink] that's it, even more frequently now. But I don't want you to allow those eyes to close until the spot has slowly come all the way down, as you come down with it.

"That's it...

"You may have noticed your arms and legs are getting heavy, as your eyelids get heavier and heavier. And as you think about how nice it would be to allow your eyes and eyelids to relax... the spot continues to sink... and I don't want you to relax all the way, or close your eyes and go all the way inside, until that spot has sunk all the way down.

"As you focus your eyes on that spot and as they become more tired and more heavy and... more fatigued... as they follow that spot down...

"As they reach the bottom, you can allow your eyes to close."

[Pause briefly]

"And closing those eyes means you can relax now... It feels so good... so peaceful... as you really let yourself relax...

"Breathing-in and out, allowing that relaxation to double throughout your entire body. Going deeper... and deeper, that's it... all the way... all the way..."

Arm Levitation

This example of an arm levitation induction is taken from a live training that I conducted a few years ago. Some points that deserve to be highlighted include the initial check that there are no medical or physical issues that would prohibit this induction.

Additionally, you will note that the induction begins

with the hypnotist seeding the idea of "subconscious movements." This serves a couple of purposes. Firstly, it elicits the expectation that such movement will soon be experienced. Secondly, it allows the client to understand the difference between a genuine hypnotic movement and them simply lifting their arm because it is suggested.

The subconscious movements are framed as both amusing and "fascinating." Further, due to the person I was working with, I described the kind of experiences we were discussing as "the clever ways our brain functions," rather than my more common description of the "power of our mind." I had a suspicion that the former would be more appealing to my client and would make them more inclined to engage with the experience.

You will also notice that words such as 'light' and 'up' are peppered throughout the induction. This may or may not be significant. I will let you judge.

> Hypnotist: "I guess I should start by asking if you have any problems with arm movement. Any shoulder issues, or mobility restraints?"
>
> Client: "No."
>
> H: "Great. And you're good with subconscious movements too? A fly goes in front of your face and you swat it without thinking, or someone throws a ball in your direction and your hand goes up to catch it, or just protect your face?"
>
> C: "Yeah."

H: "You know, it always fascinates and amuses [intentionally drops the word "me"] when that happens. I can remember, as a child, watching my mum put on make-up in the mirror, seeing her open her mouth when she was applying mascara, without even thinking about it. But I was just as bad. I used to play this computer game, where a plane had to fly up under a bridge at one point – I say plane, it might have been a helicopter, or spaceship of some kind, I really don't remember. What I do remember is that every time it flew under the bridge, I would instantly and without giving it any conscious thought, duck my head to avoid the bridge.

"It's funny how we do that sort of thing, isn't it?"

C: "Yeah, it is."

H: "I suppose it's a function of the human brain, a natural capacity we have. For our body to experience sensations created in the brain and to act on them. And we don't even need to be consciously aware of that, for it to happen. Speeds up reflexes and reactions, I suppose.

"Anyway, I'm rambling now! I do that when I get worked-up talking about the clever ways our brain functions.

"Now, all I want you to do to start is place your feet flat on the floor, with your hands resting lightly on your lap like so...

[Hypnotist demonstrates, by placing his hands gently on his thigh, fingers bent, so that there is a small but unnoticed gap under the palms. The client copies.]

H: "That's it. And your only role in all of this is to simply experience whatever you experience. So, I don't want you to fake anything, or fight anything. That's not why we're here. I want you to enjoy experiencing using your mind.

"You might want to take a nice deep breath... and let it out. Again, take another deep breath – almost willing the relaxation into your body – and let it out.

"And as you keep breathing and relaxing, relaxing and breathing, I would invite you to notice the sensations in your hands... just notice how they feel, on the top and underneath, where they are touching your legs...

"And you may already have become aware of

the differences between your hands... perhaps one hand feels warmer than the other, or one hand feels light, whilst the other hand feels heavy.

"In fact, why don't you go ahead and tell me which hand feels heavier than the other?"

C: "The right hand. The right hand definitely feels heavier."

H: "It does, doesn't it? And the left hand feels lighter. Isn't that funny? I'm glad you picked-up on that. Well, what I would invite you to do is to choose a spot on the back of your left hand and focus on it. Just let your eyes rest on that spot.

"Now, take another deep breath... fully focused on that hand... and let it out. And when you feel like you have a good sense of it, you can let your eyes softly close, whilst still imagining that you can see that spot. Continue to focus on that spot, with your eyes closed, as if you can see through your eye-lids.

[The Hypnotist begins to speak mainly on the client's inhalations.][54]

---

54 Usually, the advice is to speak when your client is *ex*haling. However, with an arm levitation, the body – and thus, the arm – naturally rises with each

"And as you allow yourself to notice everything that you notice about that hand... you can pay attention to the very end of your fingertips, where they barely make contact with the fabric of your trousers... touching your leg, ever so lightly...

"You might focus on that point where the finger makes contact with your leg... or you might notice the sensation of space... that thin minuscule layer of space that exists between the atoms of your hand and the outer edge of your leg.

"And I wonder how long it will take for you to notice that small cushion of air forming interestingly between your fingertips and your leg..."

[Spoken as the arm naturally rises on the inhalation...]

H: "That's right... And I wonder how quickly that cushion of air will expand...

"You might wonder which will begin to rise first, your fingertip, or your hand... Or you may be more focused on noticing how difficult it can

---

inhalation. Utilisation at work again!

feel to hold your hand there, as it keeps trying to move upwards a bit, as that feeling of lightness and space... gradually increases.

"It may be that you feel a push from below, or even a pull from above, as if helium balloons were tired to your wrist, pulling your hand up by the arm... It's all the same for our purposes, but it's fascinating to think about, isn't it?"

C: [Smiles]

H: "Becoming more aware now of the lift of that hand off of your lap... noticing and enjoying those tiny sensations... rising just a little bit more... almost as if it has a mind of its own.

"I don't know if you have noticed how the other hand continues to get heavier... whilst this hand is lighter... and lighter... As the rest of your body sinks deeper into that relaxation, isn't it interesting that this hand is choosing to experience the same relaxation... in such an uplifting way?"

[Hand is now levitating 2-3 inches off of the leg]

H: "And you can notice your right hand getting

heavier and heavier, or you can continue to focus on this hand that continues its uplifting journey... teaching you something deep at a subconscious level...

"That's right... And in a moment, I am going to click my fingers. And when I do so, the speed with which that hand is rising will increase. It may just continue to rise into the air, or it may begin to drift towards your face, but when I click my fingers, the speed with which that hand is rising will increase... Now."

[Clicks fingers and hand visibly begins to rise more quickly.]

H: "That's right... And I want to thank your subconscious mind for acting so powerfully on your behalf today... for giving you this experience that your conscious mind will not want to ignore. You have a powerful and wonderful mind and if you just open your eyes to see where your hand has stopped..."

[Hand stops rising roughly level with the top of her head]

H: "...you will have visible proof of just how powerful your subconscious mind really is."

C: [Client opens their eyes and laughs]

H: "And you can close your eyes now, wondering whether that hand will continue its rise, or whether it will know that now is the time to float back down…"

C: [Hand begins to move down.]

H: "…sinking and drifting down into that pleasant heavy relaxation…"

Magnetic Hands

We have already made reference to Magnetic Hands in the context of the pre-talk. It was used there as what some might describe as a convincer, or suggestibility test. We prefer to view it as a pre-cursor of hypnosis. However, here the simple yet effective phenomena is employed as a full induction.

Hopefully, it does not need stating that if you have already used Magnetic Hands in your pre-talk, it will most likely not prove effective to use it again as an induction.

This induction is incredibly flexible. It can be used as a rapid induction, where some hypnotists like to push the hands together and down as they are just about to touch. Or it can be used to demonstrate further phenomena, where the hands stick together after touching. However, the induction itself is incredibly simple and there's no reason not to get practising with this one right away.[55]

Hypnotist: "Now, just place your hands out in front of you, like this..."

[Demonstrate by placing your hands 6 inches to a shoulder width apart, palms facing each other]

"What I'm going to do in a moment - relying on the power of your imagination - is I'm going to place an incredibly powerful magnet here [touch the palm of their left hand with your fingertip, gently pushing as you do so] and here [touch the palm of their right hand with your fingertip, gently pushing the hand outwards]. When I do that, you'll begin to feel the pull between your hands..."

[Gently push their palms together, whilst saying...]

"And as your hands get closer, your eyes can close and then you'll go deeper [gently apply a little pressure on the top of their hands so that they feel a very slight downwards push] into a nice relaxing trance.

"Okay?"

---

[55] This example incorporates rehearsal, though it is not a necessary element.

HYPNOSIS WITH THE HARD TO HYPNOTISE

Client: "Yes."

H: "Good. So, just to make sure it's clear... You place your hands out... [wait for them to put their hands in the right position.] That's it. And I'll place a strong magnet here [touch the palm of their left hand with your fingertip, pushing slightly] and here [touch the palm of their right hand with your fingertip, pushing outwards slightly]. And as you become aware of that magnetic pull between your hands, your hands will begin to come together."

[Gently push their palms together, with them probably helping a little this time, whilst saying...]

"And as your hands draw closer together, you'll feel a wave of relaxation, your eyes will close and you can let your head drop forward as you sink into [apply a little pressure on the top of their hands] that nice relaxing trance.

"Got it?"

C: "Yes."

H: "Great. So, just to recap... Your hands are out... [wait for them to put their hands in the right position.] That's it. And I place a strong magnet here [touch the palm of their hand with your fingertip, pushing slightly] and here [touch the palm of their hand with your fingertip, pushing slightly].

"And as you concentrate on that magnetic field, that area between your hands, your hands begin to come together..."

[Very gently push their palms together, if they haven't already begun to do so.]

"You feel a wave of relaxation as your hands pull closer together... your eyes will close [wait for their eyes to close] as you begin to enter trance..."

[If head doesn't drop slightly forward at that point, say...] And your head can drop forward as you drop down... deeper [apply a little pressure on the top of their hands, if they haven't begun to go down] into a nice relaxing trance.

"Okay... So as you place your hands out... you can feel the power of those magnets ... [touch 1st palm and then the 2nd, with a slight push on each, as you say...] ...Now.

"Focusing on that space between the palms [Wait for movement in the hands] ...that's right. Feel the pull. You don't have to force it. You don't have to fight it. You can just enjoy the relaxation that comes over you as you see your hands coming close and closer and closer... [Wait for next movement in the hands] ...that's right.

"And as your hands touch... [Look for the slightest movement of the eyes, or a blink] your eyes can close... that's right. As the wave of relaxation floods every fibre of your body. Your hands dropping to your lap... as your head falls forwards and you sink down into that trance. Sinking, floating, drifting... more and more relaxed.

"I'm now going to count and each number I mention, and every breath you take, and every beat of your heart, doubles that relaxation you are feeling now. Focusing on my voice; all other sounds only serving to deepen that relaxation that you're already feeling, until all you can hear is my voice.

"Ten, deeper and deeper.

"Nine, every number doubling the sensation of relaxation.

"Eight, every breath taking you further down.

"Seven, every beat of your heart, deeper and deeper into that place.

"Six, more and more relaxed.

"Five, four, three, two...

"One.

"That's it. All the way into that trance... into that peaceful place."

EXERCISE

Practice using the Sinking Spot induction.

Practice the Arm Levitation induction.

Practice Magnetic Hands as a full induction.

Teach the three inductions to someone else.

Experience these three phenomenal inductions, as the hypnotee.

Then, practice them some more!

GRAHAM OLD

HYPNOSIS WITH THE HARD TO HYPNOTISE

Becoming More Hypnotic

The title of this chapter is intentionally ambiguous. Are we talking about clients increasing their own level of hypnotisability, or hypnotists being more hypnotic? The answer is a resounding, Yes!

The primary focus of this chapter will be on increasing the hypnotic responsiveness of clients. However, we will include some notes at the end of the chapter explaining how an awareness of these steps can be used by hypnotists to become more hypnotic generally.

The question of whether or not hypnotisability can be modified is hotly debated in academic circles. The topic is closely tied to the wider question of whether hypnosis is state-based or non-state-based. Unfortunately, the result of this wider debate is often one of polarisation, with neither side listening or learning much from the other. As such, I have no desire to enter into these debates here and will simply say that I am tentatively of the opinion that hypnotic responsiveness *can* be increased.[56] In fact, I would go as far as Donald Gorassini in stating, 'it cannot only be said that hypnotic responsiveness is modifiable. Hypnotic responsiveness is *highly* modifiable.'[57]

---

[56] Any readers interested in the research are encouraged to access the works in the bibliography.
[57] Quoted in Heap, *The Highly Hypnotizable Person*, p. 230. Emphasis mine.

People like Gorassini include all manner of things in their research, to increase hypnotisability. So, they include use of technological aids, an induction, level of expectation and so on. Of course, we would agree that use of an appropriate induction and increasing expectation can increase someone's likelihood to respond to hypnosis and hypnotic suggestions. That is, after all, what the majority of this book has been about! However, the practices that follow are exercises that someone can partake in both inside and outside of hypnosis to increase their general hypnotic responsiveness.

It should be noted that in none of these exercises are we aiming to teach clients how to be less analytical. We are not even asking them to put their analysis to the side for the time-being. Instead, we are working on a series of skills that may enable them to use their minds in hypnotic ways, whilst still being as wonderfully analytical as ever.

Directed Imagination

People who do not think of themselves as particularly imaginative tend not to use their imagination as often or as freely as they could, understandably. However, the first step to becoming more hypnotic is to intentionally practice using your imagination. In fact, aside from any hope of becoming more hypnotic, I am inclined to suggest that this is a good daily exercise for everyone to be doing.

Many people think of imagining something as the same as visualising an image. Whilst this appears to be the case for some people, it is not true of all of us. For some people, imagining an apple, for example, might entail little more than pretending we can see one with our eyes closed. This is one of the reasons that during a hypnosis session, I rarely instruct people to "see" something. Instead, I might say, "visualise, imagine, or pretend..." Others might say, "get a sense of...", or "become aware of..."

Directed imagination involves intentionally directing ourselves to actively imagine certain things. I usually suggest that people start with a piece of fruit. I might tell them to imagine a Lemon on their desk. I have them walk over and pick up the lemon. Then they move the lemon closer to them and then further away, noticing that it gets smaller when further away and larger when closer. I will tell them to move it to the left and the right. And that may be all for the first few days – just daily imagining a lemon.

After a few days, I would suggest that they start introducing more details. Maybe they notice the smell of the lemon more when they bring it closer. Perhaps they can see the small lumps and indentations on the surface of the fruit. And so on.

Then, if they have been imagining with their eyes closed, which most people seem to naturally do, I will encourage them to keep that lemon in their minds eye and allow it to be fixed in the mind. I might return to the initial location of the lemon on the desk and suggest that they picture it there, whilst their eyes are closed, and lock that image in place. Then, I have them keep hold of that image as they open their eyes, imagining that they can still see the lemon on the desk with their eyes open.

People have varying levels of success with this exercise, but almost everyone can improve their ability to imagine and to direct their imagination at will, given enough practice.

Mindful Absorption

This activity follows-on from the previous one. In fact, we can continue using the lemon as a focal point. We will use this as a basic exercise in mindfulness, something that almost everyone can benefit from developing.

Clients are encouraged to imagine the lemon and simply notice whatever they notice. There is nothing else for them to do but sit with the thought of the lemon. They may, as above, notice the smell or other details, but they are not intentionally directing their imagination this time. They simply sit with the lemon and notice it.

An important aspect of this exercise is learning to allow thoughts to come and go. If we are learning mindfulness – and even when we are experienced practitioners – we will find thoughts entering our mind, competing for our attention. The aim is not to reject them, or fight to keep them at a distance. Instead, practice letting them come into your head and then leave again, reminiscent of clouds passing overhead, or leaves being moved along on a stream. They come and they go. Simply let them be, as you focus on the lemon.

As people become more familiar with mindfulness, for hypnotic purposes they may want to practice becoming more absorbed in the focus of their attention. In one sense, the only real difference is an experiential one, as they find themselves drawn-in and getting lost in their focused awareness.

Useful objects for this stage of the exercise are a candle, an aquarium, or a log-fire. Practice a relaxed focus on such things, that gradually develops from mindfulness into absorption.

Some people find a bath a useful training ground for this exercise. Although they may not naturally be the kind of person who finds a bath relaxing, a number of clients have reported that having a flickering candle in their bathroom has served as a useful point of mindful focus, whilst the bath allowed their body to relax. They often report that it was only afterwards when they "snapped out of it" that they realised just how absorbed they had been in the experience.

Goal-Directed Fantasy

Within the field of hypnosis research, Goal-directed fantasies (or GDF, as they get called) are thoughts and images of situations that if they happened in the real world would produce the suggested response. A common example might be imagining helium balloons tied to your wrist, or a blast of water from a hose, underneath your palm, causing your hand to rise up into the air.

It is common for hypnotists to word their suggestions in such a way that GDFs take place. The helium balloons are a well-known example of this, as is the suggestion that magnets are causing your palms to come together. However, an interesting focus of some researchers has been the degree to which subjects might intentionally make use of GDF when responding to a hypnotic suggestion, even if they haven't been supplied by the hypnotist.[58]

---

[58] Cf. Council, Kirsch & Grant (2004). *Imagination, Expectancy, and Hypnotic Responding*. In Kunzendorf, R., Spanos, N. and Wallace, B. Hypnosis and

This is a useful idea for our purposes, because people can learn to use GDFs as a way of increasing their hypnotic responses. In fact, training subjects to do just that is the cornerstone of a number of hypnotisability modification programs used by researchers.

Those wishing to increase their hypnotic responses can make use of GDFs in two different ways. Firstly, they can add GDFs to any suggestions that they hear from a hypnotist. So, if they were told that their arm was becoming numb, they could imagine that they had sat on their arm and lost all feeling in it, or they might imagine that if had become cold after being dipped in freezing water, such that it has now become numb.

Secondly, clients can practice using GDFs outside of hypnosis. I recommend that clients practice experiencing hypnotic phenomena at home. I tell them to imagine a hypnotist has given them a suggestion for levitation, catalepsy, amnesia and so on, and then to practice imagining situations where that phenomena would be the result. Clients are encouraged to keep track of how successful they are with this, repeating the exercise until they are increasingly skilled in the use of GDF.

They are then encouraged to take this to the next stage, which involves returning to the initial suggestion without *consciously* making use of GDFs. The hope is that as their expectation of responding to suggestions has increased significantly, they will do so naturally. They may be making use of GDFs without even being aware of it, though an equally likely explanation is that the increased expectancy is the vehicle for greater responsiveness.

Imagination (pp. 41-67). Amityville, N.Y.: Baywood.

HYPNOSIS WITH THE HARD TO HYPNOTISE

Intentional Response

This exercise is most effective when practised after the client has got a handle on goal-directed fantasies. In fact, GDFs can play a role in the successful implementation of intentional responses.

This stage simply involves the client intentionally and consciously responding to suggestions. Over time, these responses will become less and less intentional until they are experienced as subconscious or automatic responses.

One way to practice this exercise is to do so in tandem with GDFs. The client may hear – or, if they are practising at home, think of – a suggestion for their arm to levitate. They then intentionally lift their arm. However, they employ GDFs so that their response does not feel completely intentional. So, they would intentionally raise their arm, but do so after having imagined it being pulled up by a large bunch of helium balloons tied to the wrist, to make it feel like it was rising by itself.

As with the previous exercise, clients are encouraged to work through all of the common hypnotic suggestions in this way. A natural way to progress is for their responses to feel less and less a result of their conscious compliance and increasingly due to the GDFs.

Rapid Relaxation

This exercise is simply a case of clients practising progressive muscle relaxation in their own time. The goal is not to use PMR as an induction, but to become familiar with the experience of relaxation. This does not need to be undertaken solely as a means to increase hypnotic responses. It is a highly valuable practice in and of itself.

Some people find it helpful to employ visualisation during this process. For example, a common choice is to imagine laying on the beach, with the Sun passing down the body. And each part of the body that the Sun passes over relaxes.

Rapid Relaxation can be developed through the use of cue-words. This is best attempted after one is very familiar with both the process of PMR and the experience of relaxing.

Use the same tension-relaxation procedure as full PMR, but work with summary groups of muscles.[59] However, this time, focus also on your breathing during both tension and relaxation. Inhale slowly as you apply and hold the tension. Then, when you let the tension go and exhale, say a cue word or phrase to yourself – something like, "Relax," or "Limp and loose." This will associate the cue word or phrase with the state of relaxation, so that eventually, through conditioning, the cue word alone will produce the relaxed state.

This takes practice, as with the full PMR routine. However, once you have learned PMR and are familiar with the feeling of muscle relaxation – and have sufficiently practised with a cue word or phrase – you will find it possible to simply think of and then relax the various muscle groups using your cue word(s).

Deep Simulation

Rather than being a separate exercise, deep simulation

---

[59] For example, 1) Lower limbs, 2) Abdomen and Chest, 3) Arms, Shoulders, and Neck and 4) the Face.

is perhaps something to be aware of when working on other techniques. The easiest way to explain it is to think of method acting, whereby an actor aims to become completely emotionally caught-up in their role.

It is tempting to say that this exercise is simply an encouragement for people to *act as if* they are good hypnotic subjects. However, in reality, it is much more than that.

Deep simulation involves taking on the mindset, the attitude, emotions and expectations of a good hypnotic subject. It means responding the way they would respond, for the reasons that they would.

As such, this exercise is possibly most useful when used in conjunction with GDFs and Intentional Responses. Growing in the skills that those exercises develop, whilst simultaneously adopting the attitude and expectations of a high hypnotisable, is a powerful way of learning to experience responses as automatic and hypnotic before they fully are.

Lessons for the Hypnotist

There are some implications from these exercises for hypnotists to be aware of. Most of these will no doubt be clear, though some may bear explicit mention.

The role of expectation has long been known to play a significant role in hypnotic responses. If someone expects a certain phenomena to take place, then both their brain and body are more likely to prepare for and work toward that end. However, we can not put the full burden for expectation on our clients.

Expectancy is not only developed through our

explanation or what will take place. Neither is it solely down to convincers or phenomena used in the pre-talk. In reality, every single thing about how we are with our clients will serve to increase or decrease expectancy.

This becomes especially relevant when we think back to our earlier discussion of some of the prejudicial labels used to dismiss clients. If we are viewing clients with an attitude of "Oh, no, it's an analytical!" we would be foolish to think that we are not projecting that for our clients to pick up on. However, if we adopt instead the expectation that they have a powerful mind, with an incredible capacity for transformation, this will be evident to the client.

The role of absorption, though not essential for hypnotic response, is something to bear in mind. I would recommend all hypnotists to become intimately aware of the experience of trance or absorption. If this is not something that comes naturally to you, then see that as a skill that you can work on. Find your trance, even if you have to seek out all manner of experiences to do so! When you are fully acquainted with the experience of absorption you will be better equipped to work with clients in a way that entices them in, through your use of words, your body language, your whole demeanour.

The idea of goal-directed fantasies is a useful one to be aware of. It is often the case that hypnotists might use GDF for their convincers of suggestibility tests (for example, employing a heavy book / helium balloon), but move towards more direct suggestions as things get more hypnotic. However, when working with someone who does not naturally think in a hypnotic way this can be a mistake. Such a client may have absolutely no idea how to have his arm float up into the air without just lifting it up himself. The idea of GDFs provide something of a stepping-stone for such clients.

Describing scenarios where the phenomena would occur, painting a vivid picture of what it would feel like if the phenomena were occurring, or providing metaphors and analogies that elicit the phenomena are not cheating. For some clients, they are the boost that they need. They may be precisely what is needed for your client to begin to learn what it means to think in a hypnotic way.

There is no reason that you can not move increasingly away from GDFs as your session progresses, or your client goes "deeper" into hypnosis, if that is your model. However, it is important to do this at a pace that does not leave your client back at the beginning, wondering why levitation worked when you were explaining hypnosis, but fails now they're actually in hypnosis!

Of course, GDFs are not limited to the traditional hypnotic phenomena. If you intend for your client to experience a state of absorption, you cannot just assume that it will happen automatically. They may have no idea how to bring that about consciously or subconsciously. Instead, you can tell stories, use metaphors, describe scenarios that evoke a state of absorption. As someone once said, seduce them into trance.

Finally, the notion of a deep simulation is particularly applicable at this point. It is of great benefit to all involved if the client can act and think as if they are a good hypnotic subject. Any way that you can orchestrate such a situation – overtly or covertly – is almost certainly going to be positive. This is equally true for the hypnotist's perception of the client.

However, deep simulation is not only for clients. As well as adopting the idea that your client is a good responder, you can immerse yourself in the idea that you are a respectful, confident, skilled, intuitive and responsive hypnotist. You can embody the emotions and values of someone who is truly excited to be working with a client who has an exceptional mind that they wield in unique ways. You can fully enter into the story of someone who cherishes the opportunity to work with people who may have been dismissed or disheartened by other so-called helpers, and is privileged to be involved in seeing that spark re-enter someone's eyes as they learn to hope again.

Becoming more hypnotic is about building skills for our clients. I would go so far as to suggest that for hypnotists it is about discovering their true calling.

EXERCISE

Take some time to familiarise yourself with the recommended exercises for clients to use to increase their hypnotisability.

Practice, to increase your own hypnotisability.

Take note of any of the exercises that seem particularly effective to you.

What can you learn from this about being more hypnotic as a practitioner?

GRAHAM OLD

Fractionation Conversation Transcript

The Fractionation Conversation is an example of an induction that is an educational process. Specifically, it covers the steps involved in going into hypnosis, allowing the client to experience each one individually. The result of this is that the client eventually goes into hypnosis, helped in no small part by the fractionation that they have experienced.

This induction meets some of the criteria of those we recommended when working with analytical clients. It gives them a process to go through, along with something to learn. However, it also meets some of the criteria from our discussion around increasing hypnotisability. This induction essentially teaches someone how to go into hypnosis. It is to be expected that the more someone experiences the steps involved, the more easily they will respond, thus potentially becoming more hypnotic.

The following induction is my version of Richard Nongard's 'Fractionation with Discussion induction.' Richard's version appears in his excellent introductory text, *Inductions and Deepeners*.[60]

My version of the Fractionation induction, is clearly inspired by Nongard's. I use his key elements, but have

---

[60] R. Nongard. (2007). *Inductions and Deepeners*. Andover, KS: Peach Tree Professional Education.

re-worded much of it and added a pre-talk that involves a number of embedded commands. Having said that, as you'll see, the beauty of this induction is that it is virtually all pre-talk!

Before you experience hypnosis, I want you to experience what it feels like to be hypnotised before you actually go into trance. How is that?

"Okay."

That's good. I'm sure you've had that experience when you're driving a Car and it's a familiar route that you know well. And after a while, you can find your conscious mind drifting off. You go into a daydream like state. You've had that, haven't you, when you get home, or you reach a certain landmark along the way and you think, "how did I get here?" And it's interesting, because what happens there is your subconscious mind takes over - but it's still you driving here.

In hypnosis, you're in a similar "day-dream" place. You know that feeling when your mind is beginning to wake you up for work or school, but your body is still enjoying being fast asleep. And you sometimes hear people speaking in your dream, when it's actually the radio, or someone calling you to wake up. Once when I was younger - and lots of people have this experience - it was getting close to the time when I would be getting ready to go off to school and learn something new and in my dream out of the blue my Mum began calling me. And in the dream I was confused but I could hear my Mum's voice, even though I wasn't consciously aware of her being there. Of course, she was in the room trying to wake me up, whilst I was enjoying my deep relaxing sleep, but could still hear her voice.

That's interesting, isn't it?

"Yeah. It's like when..." [Client went on to give a brief account of a similar experience]

I'm going to make some suggestions to you as we go through this. The suggestions will be pleasant and peaceful and probably focus on helping you to simply relax and enjoy this experience. Sounds good?

"Yep."

A friend on a course I'm on told me about a friend of hers who does hypnosis. They were at McDonalds when the waitress – who was a friend of their son – began talking to her about hypnosis. They hadn't learned what you've learned about the nature of hypnosis and wanted to know what it felt like. They said, "Close your eyes, for a second" and they did. And then she opened them and they said, "That's what hypnosis feels like."

[Client laughs]

So, you're not going to turn into a zombie, or have some kind of mystical experience. You will always be in control. You will always be able to hear my voice even if you can't hear anything else. It really is the most natural thing in the world and we all go into trance and come out again and go into trance again, countless times throughout the day. So let's start, now.

Why don't you close your eyes. Close your eyes and keep them closed for 3 or 4 seconds.

1, 2, 3, 4. Open your eyes.

That's exactly what hypnosis feels like. Did that feel strange to you?

"No."

No. It feels totally normal. Funnily enough, it almost feel like you are sitting on a chair with your eyes closed, doesn't it?

HYPNOSIS WITH THE HARD TO HYPNOTISE

"Yeah." (laughs)

Exactly. That's pretty much what hypnosis is going to feel like for you. Now I'm going to add some things to it here. I want you to close your eyes again and with your eyes closed, I want you to take a deep breath. So, go ahead and close your eyes... and take a deep breath.

Breathe in. Breathe out. And another deep breath... Breathe in. And breathe out. The amazing thing about taking a deep breath is that you are relaxing more and quickly increasing the flow of oxygen to the brain.

[Client nods.]

You can feel that already, can't you?

"Yes."

It brings you to a state of physical relaxation.

[Pause]

Now, open your eyes. How was that?

"It was good. Relaxing."

Yes. Relaxing. Good. Now. I want you to close your eyes again. We're going to add a third part to it.

With your eyes closed... breathe in. Breathe out. And again... breathe in. And out. You can probably feel your heart rate slowing down, and your breath becoming more shallow.

"Yes"

Yes. And as you relax, with each breath, simply let your mind create a mental picture of somewhere you've been that was peaceful and relaxing to you.

Create a mental picture of... somewhere you've been and look at all the colours... and maybe the people, if there are any others in your mental picture.

[pause]

Look at the scenery and the... world that surrounds you in that mental picture.

[pause]

If you are outside, you might be able to feel the cool wind or the warm air. Do you have a mental picture?

"Yes."

Good. Open your eyes again. Tell me a little bit about the picture you created. What was the picture of?

"A Beach, where we've been on holiday."

A beach. What did you become aware of in your picture as you pictured the beach?

"It's quiet. Warm. Just the sound of a few children playing. Apart from that, it's completely peaceful."

It sounds it, very peaceful.

"Yes."

It's relaxing just thinking about it, isn't it?

"Yes."

I bet that just... [wait for next time they blink]

closing your eyes and taking a few deep breaths almost takes you straight back there, doesn't it?

"Yeah, ha, just thinking about it."

It's relaxing just thinking about it. I wouldn't be at all surprised to find that when you... [wait for next time they blink] close your eyes and take a deep breath you actually already begin to float deep down into hypnosis. Would you?

"No."

Creating a mental picture of somewhere we've been that is relaxing and quiet and warm and peaceful, can help us to clear the mind of all of the stress and tension that we are carrying around with us... [wait for next time they blink] That's good.

Another great way to relax is to let all of the muscles in our body go. In hypnotherapy, we often call this progressive muscle relaxation and people find that as they let go, it really helps them go into trance.

So you might want to just uncross your legs. Let your arms go. And just... [wait for next time they blink] relax.

Take another deep breath. Breathe in. Breathe out.

[Therapist has been blinking in time with the subject and now slows that down. As the client blinks slowly as well, say...]

That's it.

And as your eyes close... That's it... That means you are ready to relax even deeper.

Take a deep breath. Breathe in... and breathe out. Breathe in... and breathe out.

And as you do, your mind can open more and more to that peaceful and relaxing place you've been before.

[Client's head drops forward]

And as you go into that deeper and deeper process of [said slowly] re-lax-ation you might find your head tilting forward... and that's fine. That's just your body agreeing to your mind's decision to let go and relax.

As you create a mental picture in your mind of somewhere relaxing and quiet... somewhere warm and peaceful... I want you to allow your body to experience a tremendous amount of relaxation.

[pause. Wait for out-breath] That's it.

Feel your heart rate slowing. Feel the oxygen being pumped throughout your body. Simply let every muscle in your body go limp and loose.

[pause]

You can start with the muscles in your face, your temples... around your eyes...

Relax the muscles in the neck and back. Anywhere you feel tension, simply let that tension disappear... as you relax.

[pause]

Imagine the sensation of relaxation in your body doubling with each breath you take.

Not only can the body... [wait for out-breath] relax, but the mind can relax, as well. And as the mind relaxes, the wonderful thing... is that it's impossible not to let go of stress and tension. You cannot be as relaxed as you are now and not let go of that. Breathing-in relaxation. Breathing-out any tension. Your relaxation doubling with each breath you take.

In your mind, let your thoughts become absorbed in the scenery of that warm, relaxing place that you have created.

[pause]

You will always be able to hear the words that I use, but as your mind becomes absorbed in the imagery you've created... perhaps you won't focus on the words that I use, but only those words that your subconscious needs to hear.

[pause]

As you relax, perhaps there are outside noises or distractions... if you hear anything... that keeps your mind from being able to focus on what is important and relaxing in that image you've created... simply use that noise as a reminder to bring your attention and your awareness back to the place of peace and tranquillity that you have created.

[pause]

This is hypnosis that you are enjoying, right now.

You could think to yourself, "If I wanted to open my eyes, I could."

And, you are right. But you don't do that because it feels so good to simply relax... and feel your mind and body... become one, as you allow yourself to experience... total peace...

EXERCISE

In what other ways might you incorporate fractionation in your induction?

What do you think of the idea of using the Induction as a teaching process?

Can you think of other ways to be interactive in your inductions?

Practice using the Fractionation Conversation.

Does the conversation and participation seem to interrupt trance, or serve to deepen it?

GRAHAM OLD

Summary

We have demonstrated a number of inductions and mentioned yet more in passing:

- My Friend John
- The Auto Dual Induction
- Confusion Induction
- Sensory Overload / Overlap
- The Fake Induction
- The Modified Wicks Induction
- The Sinking Spot
- Arm Levitation
- Fractionation Conversation
- Magnetic Hands
- The Elman Induction
- PHRIT
- Thain Wrist-lift

However, it is essential to add that the key to working with clients that we may struggle to hypnotise is not finding the perfect induction. Contrary to what some others may teach, I do not believe that e.g. a Confusion Induction, or Sensory Overload are *the* secret magic bullets that will topple any analytical or resistant client.

Instead, the key is utilisation. Meeting your client where they are at, respecting the way that their mind appears to be working, and responding accordingly are the key. These inductions are only included as examples of some of the principles we have discussed.

As we have covered so much ground, including more theory – along with more examples – than we usually do, it may be helpful to provide a brief summary of some of the points that have been made.

Start as you mean to go on

We discussed the importance of setting-off as you intend to continue. We provided an example of a pre-talk that may do this and a reminder of the need to set expectations from the very beginning.

Resistance

One of the most important sections of the book was an appeal to reconsider the way we understand and speak of resistance. Following the example set by Solution-focused Therapists and the world of Motivational Interviewing, we emphasised resistance as an interactional occurrence. This removes any judgement, or assumptions, from clients that may seem to be resistant. Instead, it inspires the hypnotist to respond flexibly and adapt what he is doing to the blockage that appears to exist in their interaction with the client.

HYPNOSIS WITH THE HARD TO HYPNOTISE

Utilisation

The key approach repeated throughout this book is utilisation. Use whatever your client gives you, responding to them as an individual and not giving-up, or making negative assessments of them, if things do not proceed as per normal.

When looking at situations of resistance and when we considered working with so-called analytical subjects, we emphasised the need to accept what your client brings to the table. We discouraged trying to work against the way that your client seemed to be acting and thinking, as this only creates more resistance. Instead, we recommended respecting the way their minds functioned and adapting our work accordingly.

Analytical

We rejected the common practice of labelling certain clients as "analyticals," or "analytical subjects." We suggested that this was an unhelpful nominalisation and a static limiting description of people who were actually dynamic and multi-contextual beings.

We further suggested that not everyone who is presumed to be "an analytical" actually is. Often someone is assumed to be an over-thinker, simply because they do not shut-down when the hypnotist expects them to. We introduced the concept of 'hypnotic thinking' and then wondered if some of those who were labelled as analytical may simply not intuitively think in a very hypnotic way.

There is no denying that some people do seem to prefer a more analytical thinking-style, even if this is only at certain times and places. We offered the suggestion that analysis itself can be a form of trance. This may mean that one way to work with such clients is not to work so hard to induce trance, but instead to aim to redirect the trance that already exists.

Confusion

We had a lot to say about confusion! However, I hope that we were fair in presenting some of the common teachings regarding confusion. We shared the idea that confusion causes someone to retreat into trance to escape the uncertainty. We also mentioned various types of confusion, before providing an example Confusion Induction transcript.

We then took some time to explore Stephen Gilligan's approach to confusion, providing a framework for putting it into practice. This involved discussing the useful idea of Milton Erickson's that confusion provides a 'dimming of outer reality.'

Then we questioned the common view that confusion is *the* tool to use with resistant and/or analytical clients. We suggested that such a practice was neither necessary, or particularly therapeutic. However, we finished that slaying of sacred cows with an appreciation of kinaesthetic confusion.

Phenomena is Essential

One point that has been made throughout the book is that phenomena is essential. If anything must take the place of confusion as *the* go-to tool for working with so-called analytical clients, our vote goes to hypnotic phenomena.

We provided three examples of inductions that have phenomena at their core, as well as the Modified Wicks induction, which may be thought of as working with kinaesthetic confusion.

Becoming more Hypnotic

Finally, we discussed some ways that it may be possible for someone to learn to be more hypnotic. This involved exercises and practices to increase subconscious responses, absorption and imagination/fantasy capacity.

The underlying motivation for all of the above has been to remove the fear and prejudice that often comes from working with clients who are considered analytical, resistant, or otherwise hard to hypnotise. The aim has been to ignite a fresh excitement and flexibility to work with a client-base who may provide challenges that stretch us, but ultimately shape us into more effective, attentive and respectful therapists.

EXERCISE

Continue to practice the various inductions and principles taught in this book.

This book can not guarantee that you will master working with the 'hard to hypnotise' any more than a DVD on playing the Guitar can secure you a sell-out tour at Wembley Stadium.

Practice.

Practice.

Practice.

And then practice some more!

Why not join the How to do Inductions facebook group to discuss how you're getting on? Just search for us!

FAQ and Troubleshooting

Do you subscribe to the HMI models of suggestibility?

The Hypnosis Motivational Institute teach a model of suggestibility that categorises people as being Emotionally, Physically, or Intellectually Suggestible. People can obviously be a combination of these, but will tend to prioritise one in particular.

This is not a model that I subscribe to, nor one that we teach on our courses. Whilst having some merit, it appears to me to be another example of personality profiling. I have not personally found that to be a necessary or helpful tool in my therapeutic hypnosis work.

I failed with the Auto Dual Induction

The thing that the transcript does not capture very well is the fact that this induction is an exercise in pacing and leading. There is no point in saying, "Five... My breathing is deep, gentle and rhythmic," if their breathing is not yet deep and rhythmic, or at least heading in that direction. In that case, you would begin by saying something like, "With each breath I take, I notice that I can relax more."

Similarly, you can incorporate whatever responses they

give you. If you notice their head drop forward, as it tires, only for them to lift it up again, you might say, "Two... My head is becoming heavy, as I become drowsier and sleepier."

If you feel that you need to weight things more in your favour, you can be explicit by telling them that when you say "deep sleep now" it is an indication for them to take themselves inside.[61] That way, not only do you give them nothing to resist – by having them give themselves the instructions – but you also ensure that the actual point at which they go into hypnosis is also down to them.

Are you not just being picky about Confusion?

That's certainly possible. However, I am not suggesting that no one else should use confusion, or that they must share my view on it. I am simply saying that *the way I see confusion commonly used* does not fit with my commitment to Therapeutic Inductions.

If you feel that you can incorporate confusion into your inductions in a way that respects the individuality of your clients and acknowledges their unique gifts, by all means go for it.

How can confusion be the basis of all hypnotic induction techniques?

Erickson wrote in *Hypnotic Realities* that 'the basis of

---

[61] This idea is behind the simple but effective Deeper Sleep Induction. See http://www.howtodoinductions.com/inductions/sleep

good hypnotic induction is confusion.'[62] That certainly seems like a bold claim, so what could he have meant by it?

It is important to recognise how Erickson defines confusion in *Hypnotic Realities*, if we are to understand this statement in context. Erickson is thinking about confusion in a broad sense that we might describe as 'uncertainty about reality.' This incorporates more than the bewilderment that we often think of as characterising confusion. It is 'something that breaks up their reality orientation.'

The confusion Erickson is speaking of is a result of the 'dimming of outer reality.' Understood in that way, it may make more sense why someone could consider it to be the basis of all induction techniques. This is confusion, uncertainty, or doubt about reality and our relationship to it. It is a suspicion that the usual rules do not apply – and that sense that reality may not be what it once was seems to me a fairly good description of the hypnotic experience.

I never seem able to get an arm levitation

It is important to remember that an arm levitation is a pace and lead induction. It is not a series of steps that you go through, regardless of what your client is experiencing. Instead, you adapt what you say depending on how your client is responding.

One benefit of the induction that was shared in this book is that the client has their eyes closed. This means

---

[62] Erickson, *Hypnotic Realities*, p. 107.

that if all else fails, you can rely upon your client's imagined levitation and proceed as if that was the intended outcome all along. You may be surprised by how many clients cannot tell if their arm is physically lifting, or how high it has got, when their eyes are closed. You might then have them imagine the arm floating down again, allowing themselves to "float down with it" into a state of trance.

The initial placement of the arm on their lap can effect how likely it is to rise. When you are asking someone to place their hand on their lap, it can be useful to emphasise that they are to do so lightly. You may also want to tell them to have their hand slightly raised, so that the fingers are effectively hanging-down. In such cases, it is also useful to ensure that your client's elbows are not leaning against their body. In this way, you are stacking the deck in your favour, as they are already elevating their hands and engaging their muscles to keep them in place.

Additionally, you can employ the trick that Erickson relied on occasionally, which is to lift the arm slightly to start-off the levitation. Some clients will not be aware that you are literally expecting their arm to rise, or their arm and muscles may be in such a position that levitation is unlikely. Thus, initiating the lift for them allows them to engage with the idea.

Another option is to switch tacks and turn their attention instead to the heavy hand on the other side. (This can actually work quite well with the "imagined" hand left floating in the air.) You can then proceed to utilise the heaviness of their hand and morph it into a hand-stick, with the hand too heavy to lift off of their leg.

HYPNOSIS WITH THE HARD TO HYPNOTISE

What about people with Autism?

Dr. Stephen Store once wrote, "if you have met one person with autism, you have met one person with autism." It is therefore essential not to presume that each autistic person we work with will respond exactly the same way as every other autistic person.

So, the first thing to do when working with someone on the autism spectrum is to calibrate to the individual in front of you. There are a number of things to be aware of when working with an autistic individual, including their level of concrete / abstract thinking, any sensory issues and their special interests.

With that caveat out of the way, most of the time I would recommend simply following the rest of the advice in this book when working with people with autism. In brief, the only additional points I would want to emphasise are:

- Be aware of sensory issues[63]
- Embrace a spirit of experimentation
- Utilise their interests
- Explain a variety of valid responses
- Employ Active inductions
- Do not rely on trance
- Avoid trying to use confusion – it is annoying!

Of course, inducing hypnosis with someone is only the beginning. If this is a community of clients you expect to

---

63 Generally, you will want to avoid any kind of sensory overload induction. Though sensory overload is not a problem for some people with autism, it is a real issue for many. Anything that simulates it is unlikely to be welcomed.

be working with therapeutically, I would recommend familiarising yourself with the lived experience of people with an autistic condition. A good place to start is the article *Working Hypnotically with Children on the Autism Spectrum* by Diane Yapko.[64] Some further resources are listed in the appendices.

What is Chevreul's Pendulum and how can I use it?

Chevreul was a French chemist in the 1800s. He investigated the apparently occult phenomenon of the pendulum, seeking to find a plausible scientific explanation. He found that the pendulum effect is due to the body responding as if imagined actions were real.

If you intend to demonstrate Chevreul's Pendulum to yourself or your clients, the first step will be acquiring or making a "pendulum." So, take a small weight - a ring, a lead fishing weight, or so on - and attach it to a piece of string, roughly 30cm in length. It is often recommended that you attach something like a button to the other end, to make it easier to hold. Then, simply follow these steps:

1: Take a piece of paper and draw a large circle in the middle (30-45cm diameter). Then draw a large cross through the circle, dividing it equally into four quarters. You will be left with something that resembles the cross-hairs of an optical instrument or gun-sight.

2: Seated at a table, hold the string between your thumb and forefinger, with the pendulum weight hanging

---

[64] The article is currently available online at https://yapko.com/wp-content/uploads/2016/04/Working-Hypnotically-with-Children-on-the-Autism-Spectrum1.pdf

straight down. The end of the pendulum should be 1-2cm above the centre of the cross. With your arm tension-free, hold the pendulum as still as possible.

3: While holding the pendulum still, just imagine what it would feel like if the pendulum started to swing along the vertical axis. Imagine it is swinging and you are watching it swing vertically along the line. Do not consciously make it swing. Within a few moments, you may find that the pendulum starts to swing. It is likely that it will start with small swings and then increase.

4: Then imagine what it would feel like if the pendulum started to swing along the horizontal axis. Imagine it is swinging, but don't do anything consciously to make it swing. After a while, the pendulum will start to swing horizontally.

5: Now, imagine the pendulum swinging around the circle, first clockwise and then counter-clockwise...

Chevreul's pendulum can be used to show your clients that their mind is able to communicate with their body. They did not consciously swing the pendulum, yet they were imagining it and their body responded by making tiny micro-movements which caused the pendulum to swing.

This can be used therapeutically, to engage in "subconscious communication" outside of trance. For example, you might want to designate the horizontal axis as "Yes," and the vertical axis as "No." Depending on how you frame it, you are then able to ask questions of your client's subconscious mind and have them provide subconscious responses.

Can you elaborate on your Sensory Overlap Induction?

As the term implies, a Sensory Over*load* Induction is intended to overwhelm someone (usually analytical clients). The goal is to overload them with sensory input, to such a degree that they essentially burst and jump into trance as a way to break free. This is not a way that I am particularly keen to work with people.

It may have been my work with individuals on the autistic spectrum, but I do not think that sensory overload is something we should take lightly. It can be an uncomfortable and distressing experience. So, if I think that a similar approach would ever be useful, I opt for a sensory overlap instead. This is essentially a gentle and less explosive version of a sensory overload induction.

I often think of it as a conductor introducing additional instruments to the sound of one haunting violinist. At first, the sounds may complement the violin, but after a while it becomes unwelcome noise as more and more sounds are added. Imagine listening to that cacophony and having the power to reverse the actions of the conductor, removing each additional sound that was added, one by one. As you get down to 3 or 4 instruments, your ears will hone in on the sound of the violent, seeking it out. Then, as the remaining additional instruments are removed, the sound of that violin will become more prominent and desirable. Finally, there is the relief that is experienced as you are left with that lone violin, focusing on that sound.

There is no burst or overload. No unpleasant experience to be escaped from. Instead, you take a skill that the client has – to think and analyse what is taking place – and you build on it. You accentuate that skill and then you relax it. You are effectively pacing and leading from one state, up into an accelerated state of multi-focus and then working backwards into a state of singular focus on the first sound that was heard – the hypnotist's voice.

Some people are definitely resistant!

You might be right. However, I think it would be good if hypnotists and therapists did not jump to this as their primary assumption when things do not seem to be going as planned.

The truth is, even if I felt that someone was resistant – for example, working with a client in a statutory setting – it serves me well to reframe that. That is, I get more out of my clients if I expect the best from them. Any 'resistance' that is encountered is understood to be a result of the dynamic encounter between us, rather than an attitudinal trait of the client. Sure, it may not always be true, but more often than not, it seems to work itself out if I proceed as if it is.

Finally, if you are convinced that you have a client who is undeniably and unvaryingly resistant, my only question would be, why are you working with them? If someone really does not want to be hypnotised, why are you even trying?

You imply that over-thinking is not an issue. However, how would you work with someone who insisted that they cannot go into hypnosis because they can't stop thinking about what I'm saying?

In such a situation, my first step would be to ask them why they think they need to stop thinking about what I was saying. It seems likely that expectations have not been managed as well as they might have been, leaving this client to think that they are somehow doing something which inhibits hypnosis. Yet, they are not.

Then, it's possible that I might use a sensory overlap induction, with a positive slant so there was an implicit praise for their ability to think about everything I was saying. This could then be extended to include the slowing-down of the induction, inviting them to think carefully about my words, assisting them to focus on the declining number of items I am bringing to their attention.

However, depending on what I was picking-up from the client, I suspect that I would want to proceed by going straight for some phenomena. I may even make use of something as simple as the Balloon and Book test.[65] I would emphasise, during the activity, that I wanted them to pay close attention to my words, as that would be key to them being able to engage with them.

Following that, I may be tempted to remind them that I want them to pay deep attention to everything that I say. I don't want merely surface-level attention like some clients provide. Given the strength of their mind, I expect them to pay deep attention, which means really listening

---

65 See, for example, http://www.howtodoinductions.com/exercises/balloon.

to my words, holding on to them, considering them from all angles and engaging with them. I might explain how some clients might hear a word like "Blackbird" and simply hear the word, or think of a picture of a blackbird. But I was expecting more from them. I want them to hear the word, think about the meaning of the word (who chose such a lazy description?!), see or imagine seeing a blackbird, maybe in flight, maybe on a branch, hear the song of the blackbird, perhaps even see it fly away afterwards, hearing the sound of its wings on the wind. And that's all at the same time as wondering why I said the word "Blackbird" and paying deep attention to what I said before and afterwards. Some clients will take this as a challenge – and become the most wonderfully engaging hypnotees in the process. Others will concede that they don't think about what I'm saying that much after all.

As with the general advice in this book, I would not be seeking to question, challenge or confront the way such clients minds work. Instead, I would want to accept it and utilise it, building on the unique skill-set they bring to the encounter.

How can I get better with the Modified Wicks Induction?

Practice.

Consistent success with the Modified Wicks usually comes down to timing. (Other issues like congruency and confidence may come in to play, but assuming they are sorted, the issue is likely to be timing.) There are two ways that mastery of the timing involved will improve your work with this induction.

Firstly, the extension of the arm. There is the question of your verbal timing as you are lifting up the arm. You need to time it so that you are saying, "hold it" as you are releasing your hold on the hand. This is intended to provoke a confusion in them as they wonder – consciously or subconsciously – if you mean for them to hold their breath, or their arm, or both.

Then there is the timing involved in how you left go of, or release some of your support for the arm. When I am bringing the arm to full extension, I imagine myself "placing" the hand in its position. I actually think of a hook that I am placing the hand on to, which actually entails placing the hand ever so slightly higher than its final resting place and letting it drop down into place a millimetre or two. This may be a fine detail that you can pay no heed to, as I am told by those who have seen me using this induction, that you cannot tell I am "hooking" the arm in this way. However, it is certainly in my mindset and I presume that the client gains a sense that the arm will stay up from how I place it.

Secondly, there is the timing involved in how the arm comes down. The "patter" you use can have a great effect on how the arm comes down. Notice some of the terminology used:

> "In a moment, your arm will slowly begin to float down to your lap. As it comes down, you will feel yourself going more and more deeply into hypnosis. But I don't want you to go all the way in, until that hand has come to rest."

Not only is it explicit that the arm is to come down

slowly, but you emphasise that the hand coming to rest will coincide with the client going into hypnosis. This latter point is then repeated as the arm continues its descent.

Repeated experience with the induction is key to gaining confidence and good timing, particularly as far as the patter during the descent is concerned. So, as I said, practice is the key.

That's all well and good, but no matter what I say or do, their arm always comes down too quickly during the Modified Wicks.

This is actually the reason that Graham Wicks prefers to control the hand as it comes down, regardless of the response of his client, instead of letting it come down on its own. So, that is always an option. However, my personal opinion – and the reason why I developed the modified version – is that this misses out on the benefit of the client experiencing catalepsy and an apparently subconscious movement of the arm.

If I am working with someone and their arm is coming down too quickly, I may attempt to intervene early and remind them that, "the arm comes down only as quickly as you go into hypnosis." I may at times adapt the words to say something like, "coming down only as quickly as you are willing to go into hypnosis."[66]

At times, you might find that the arm still comes down

---

[66] The only thing to be aware of with that second wording is that some clients may not think you mean for them to go into hypnosis then. They may just think you mean that if they are willing to go into hypnosis quickly, they should lower their hand quickly. It's a rare misunderstanding, but it's not completely unknown.

too quickly. Then, I would recommend simply moving to the other side of your client and saying, "And now this side..." They will have no idea that you did not intend to use both arms all along!

I had one trainee who found that his client's second arm came down just as quickly (which is to be somewhat expected). So, he simply acted as if he had always planned to do a second round and went back to the first arm. As he lifted up that first arm for the second round, he said, "And even deeper this time, even slower, as you enter fully into that process..." They responded well to this arm, but he still went ahead and used the other arm for a second time, which served as an effective deepener. A wonderful example of utilisation!

Any tips for Magnetic Hands (as a full induction)?

If you do not have success with magnetic hands more often than not, it may be worth re-examining what *you* are doing during the induction.

Check the position of your client's elbows before you start. If their arms are rigidly against their sides, it may make movement less likely. I normally position their hands so that the elbows are slightly in front or to the side of their body.

Confirm their experience with magnets. It may sound like a silly point, but if you do not see any sign of recognition when you are describing the magnets, double-check your client's knowledge of magnets. Ideally, you do not just want someone who knows theoretically what they do. You want someone who has held magnets and felt them pulling towards each other.

HYPNOSIS WITH THE HARD TO HYPNOTISE

To go along with the previous point, you might sometimes want to mention pressure from outside the hands as well. Some people suggest a large elastic band around the outside of the hands, pushing them together.

A really useful tip, that I now use whenever I go for the full induction, is to push the hands slightly as you are applying the magnets. This is a natural action, as you are placing the magnets onto the palms. However, it also introduces the experience of movement. For the first time, the hands are not fixed in their position. The reason this is such an effective tip is that when you push the hands out, they naturally move back in. So, not only are they now able to move, but they have also moved inwards in response to the placing of the magnets. I thoroughly recommend this little addition.

The final element that I include when performing the full induction is the use of rehearsal. As I demonstrate what will take place, I move the clients hand in 2 or 3 times. It might surprise you when you first start using this, how many people are already responding to you on the second or third rehearsal. Sometimes, you will even see people demonstrating signs of going into trance!

Finally, if none of this improves your success rate with the induction, consider starting with magnetic fingers.[67] That has a hidden physiological aspect, which means that all things being equal, the fingers *will* come together. Some people benefit greatly from experiencing that first and seeing that they can respond to hypnotic suggestions.

---

67 See, for example, http://www.howtodoinductions.com/exercises/fingers.

I'm not convinced that hypnotisability can be increased?

You may well be right. However, I would suggest that the research currently seems to suggest that hypnotic suggestibility can be modified, but it is true that there are arguments on both sides. This is a very live issue in hypnosis research and it has implications for wider questions and theoretical models. Thus, it will be some time before we see a definitive and universally accepted answer to this question.

I would add that I have worked with a number of people – myself included – who have wanted to increase the quality of their hypnotic responses. This has not been 100% successful across the board, yet there have been some definite improvements for most people. If nothing else, the simple act of coming back for repeated sessions and being hypnotised a number of times, seems to have a positive effect on some client's hypnotisability.

Where can I learn more?

www.howtodoinductions.com

As you would expect, we would recommend our free inductions site as the premier website for learning about inductions.

Our web-site offers transcripts of various inductions, from classics like the Progressive Muscle Relaxation to the Bandler Handshake and others. New inductions are added - and annotated - regularly, but only after they have been assessed as useful and achievable for beginners and experts alike.

www.briefhypnosis.com

Brief Hypnosis run live trainings in hypnosis and Therapeutic Inductions, offering hands-on experience in creating solution-focused inductions on-the-fly. You will learn principles and techniques that are not often taught elsewhere, which will take your confidence, creativity and client-base to completely new levels.

Sign-up for the newsletter at howtodoinductions.com to stay informed.

EXERCISE

Contact us at www.howtodoinductions.com if you have any ongoing questions which have not been answered.

Or join the How to do Inductions facebook group to chat with others.

Appendix A - Therapeutic Story-telling

Acquainting yourself with the following books will be of value as you are beginning to develop your use of therapeutic story-telling.

Gordon, D. (1978). *Therapeutic metaphors*. Cupertino, Calif.: Meta Publications.

Lankton, C. and Lankton, S. (1989). *Tales of enchantment*. New York: Brunner/Mazel.

Owen, N. (2001). *The magic of metaphor*. Crown House Publishing.

Owen, N. (2004). *More magic of metaphor*. Carmarthen, Wales, U.K.: Crown House Pub.

Parkinson, R. (2009). *Transforming Tales: How Stories Can Change People*. Jessica Kingsley Publishers.

Rosen, S. (1991). *Teaching Tales of Milton H. Erikson*. New York: W W Norton & Co Ltd.

Stoddard, J. and Afari, N. (2014). *The big book of ACT metaphors*. New Harbinger Publications: Oakland.

Thomson, Linda. (2005). *Harry the Hypnopotamus: Metaphorical Tales for the Treatment of Children.* Crown House Publishing: Carmarthen, Wales.

Appendix B - Autism Resources

The following resources are useful if you plan to work with people with autism.

Attwood, T. (2008). *The Complete Guide to Asperger's Syndrome*. London: Jessica Kingsley Publishers.

Attwood, T., Evans, C. R. & Lesko, A. (2014). *Been There. Done That. Try This!: An Aspie's Guide to Life on Earth*. London: Jessica Kingsley Publishers.

Attwood, T. & Garnett, M. (2016). *Exploring Depression, and Beating the Blues: A CBT Self-Help Guide to Understanding and Coping with Depression in Asperger's Syndrome*. London: Jessica Kingsley Publishers.

Bogdashina, O. (2003). *Sensory Perceptual Issues in Autism and Asperger Syndrome*. London: Jessica Kingsley Publishers.

Goldberg, L. (2013). *Yoga Therapy for Children*

with *Autism and Special Needs*. New York: W. W. Norton & Company.

Grandin, T. (2014). *The Autistic Brain*. London: Rider.

Karim, K., Ali, A. and O'Reilly, M. (2013). *A Practical Guide To Mental Health Problems In Children With Autistic Spectrum Disorder*. London: Jessica Kingsley Pub.

Lipsky, D. (2011). *From Anxiety to Meltdown: How Individuals on the Autism Spectrum Deal with Anxiety, Experience Meltdowns, Manifest Tantrums, and How You Can Intervene Effectively*. London: Jessica Kingsley Publishers.

Mattelin, E. & Volckaert, H. (2017). *Autism and Solution-focused Practice*. London: Jessica Kingsley Publishers.

Phifer, L. & Crowder, A. (2017). *CBT Toolbox for Children and Adolescents: Over 220 Worksheets & Exercises for Trauma, ADHD, Autism, Anxiety, Depression & Conduct Disorders*. Ashland: Pesi Publishing & Media

Prizant, B. M. (2015). *Uniquely Human: A Different Way of Seeing Autism*. New York: Simon & Schuster.

Purkis, J., Goodall, E. and Nugent, J. (2016). *The Guide to Good Mental Health on the Autism Spectrum*. London: Jessica Kingsley Publishers.

Searle, R. (2010). *Asperger Syndrome in Adults: A Guide To Realising Your Potential*. London: Sheldon Press.

Sicile-Kira, C. (2014). *Autism Spectrum Disorder: The Complete Guide to Understanding Autism*. New York: Penguin Group.

Silberman, S. (2016). *NeuroTribes: The Legacy of Autism and How to Think Smarter About People Who Think Differently*. Crows Nest NSW: Allen & Unwin.

Torrance, J. (2018). *Therapeutic Adventures with Autistic Children: Connecting through Movement, Play and Creativity*. London: Jessica Kingsley Publishers.

Wylie, P. (2014). *Very Late Diagnosis of Asperger Syndrome*. London: Jessica Kingsley Publishers.

GRAHAM OLD

Bibliography

Bandler, R., & Grinder, J. (1975). *Patterns of the hypnotic techniques of Milton H. Erickson, M.D. (Vol. 1)*. Cupertino, CA: Meta Publications, p. 196

Battino, R & South, T. (2005). *Ericksonian Approaches: A Comprehensive Manual*. Carmarthen: Crown House Publishing.

D'Mello, S., Lehman, B., Pekrun, R. & Graesser, A. (2014). *Confusion can be beneficial for learning*. Learning and Instruction, 29, 153-170.

de Shazer, S. (1984), *The Death of Resistance*. Family Process, 23: 11–17.

de Shazer, S. *Resistance Revisited* in Contemporary Family Therapy (1989) 11: 227.

Dolan, Y. M. (1985). *A Path with a Heart: Ericksonian utilization with resistant and chronic clients*. New York: Brunner/Mazel.

Erickson, M., Rossi, E. and Ryan, M. (1998). *Creative choice in Hypnosis*. London: Free Association Books.

Erickson, M. and Rossi, E. (1980). *The Nature of Hypnosis and Suggestion* (The Collected Papers of Milton H. Erickson, Vol. 1). New York: Irvington Publishers.

Erickson, *The Confusion Technique in Hypnosis*. The American Journal of Clinical Hypnosis, January, 1964, 6, 183-207.

Erickson, M. H. (1976). *Hypnotic Realities: The Induction of Clinical Hypnosis and Forms of Indirect Suggestion.* New York: Irvington Publishers.

Heap, M., Brown, R. and Oakley, D. (2004). *The Highly Hypnotizable Person*. Hove, East Sussex: Brunner-Routledge.

Havens, R. and Walter, C. (2015). *Hypnotherapy scripts*. London: Routledge.

Gandhi B, et al. *Does 'hypnosis' by any other name smell as sweet? The efficacy of 'hypnotic' inductions depends on the label 'hypnosis'.*

Consciousness and Cognition, Volume 14, Issue 2, June 2005, Pp. 304-315.

Gearan P., Schoenberger N. E & Kirsch I. (1995). *Modifying Hypnotizability: A New Component Analysis*, International Journal of Clinical and Experimental Hypnosis, 43:1, pp. 70-89.

Gilligan, S. G. (1987). *Therapeutic Trances: The Co-Operation Principle In Ericksonian Hypnotherapy.* New York: Routledge.

Gilligan, S. G. (1987). *The Legacy of Milton H. Erickson: Selected Papers of Stephen Gilligan.* New York: Routledge.

Lankton, S., & Lankton, C. (1983). *The Answer Within: A Clinical Framework of Ericksonian Hypnotherapy.* New York: Brunner Mazel Publishers, Inc.

Matthews WJ, Kirsch I, Mosher D. *Double hypnotic induction: an initial empirical test.* Journal of Abnormal Psychology. 1985 Feb;94(1):92-5.

Nongard, R. (2007). *Inductions and Deepeners: Styles and Approaches for Effective Hypnosis.* Andover, KS: Peach Tree

Professional Education.

O'Hanlon, B. (2009). *A Guide to Trance Land*. New York: WM. Norton.

Old, G. (2016). *The Elman Induction*. Milton Keynes: Plastic Spoon.

Old, G. (2018). *The Hypnotic Handshakes*. Milton Keynes: Plastic Spoon.

Old, G. (2014). *Mastering the Leisure Induction*. Milton Keynes: Plastic Spoon.

Old, G. (2016). *Revisiting Hypnosis: The Principles and Practice of Post-Hypnotic Re-induction Training for Anchoring, Post-hypnotic Suggestions and Inductions*. Milton Keynes: Plastic Spoon.

Spanos, N. and Wallace, B. (2004). *Hypnosis and Imagination*. Amityville, N.Y.: Baywood.

Stanger, T., Tucker, C. & Morgan, J. *The Impact of a Confusion Technique on Hypnotic Responsivity in Low-Susceptible Subjects*. American Journal of Clinical Hypnosis, Volume 38, 1996 - Issue 3.

Yapko, M. (2014). *Essentials of hypnosis*. New York: Routledge.

GRAHAM OLD

About the Author

Graham Old is a Solution-focused Hypnotist from the United Kingdom. A Graduate of Spurgeon's College, London and the University of Wales, Graham is a former University Chaplain and Community Pastor and remains an active participant of local peace and justice campaigns. He has experience as a Father's Worker and Assistant Social Worker, as well as working in private clinical practice and running the most popular inductions site on the web.

Graham is a popular conference speaker, writer and trainer, with over two decades experience teaching meditation and self-hypnosis. He is an insightful presence in contemporary hypnosis and the developer of the acclaimed *Therapeutic Inductions* approach.

Printed in Poland
by Amazon Fulfillment
Poland Sp. z o.o., Wrocław